"In a world increasingly shaped by environmental and social challenges, *Teaching Environmental Justice in the Elementary Classroom* offers the essential guidance educators need to begin crucial conversations with our youngest learners. This thoughtful and practical resource empowers teachers to cultivate layered leadership through nurturing students who not only understand the interconnection between people and places but who also grow into compassionate, informed community members. Rooted in care and courage, this book equips educators to foster a generation ready to engage critically and empathetically with the world around them."

Dr. Whitney Aragaki, *High School Science Teacher and co-author of* Place-Based Science Teaching: Connecting Students to Curriculum, Community, and Caring for Our Planet

"Through personal narrative, real classroom vignettes, and practical strategies, this book makes it easy for educators to embrace environmental justice in their classrooms. It's a must-read for all elementary teachers ready to reimagine education as a tool for systemic change."

Margaret Wang-Aghania, *Executive Director & Co-Founder of SubjectToClimate*

"Kimi Waite's book is a valuable support for elementary teachers who are ready to help their students develop understanding, and cultivate a commitment to action, in relation to the most pressing local and global matters. Don't shy away from this difficult topic; help your students move forward with knowledge, hope, and geographic thinking."

Thomas Herman, *Executive Director, National Council for Geographic Education*

"In this essential book, Waite equips educators with tools to teach environmental justice through four guiding principles, historical context, and national standards. Featuring ready-to-use activities, writing prompts, and links, it's both practical and inspiring—offering a replicable model for teaching intersectionality and rethinking environmental heroes. A must-have resource!"

Justin Kaput, *K-12 Science Coordinator, Suffield Public Schools*

"In the current precarious political climate where educators fear "woke" retaliation, Waite provides tangible strategies for experiential, student-centered learning that can inspire positive change through genuine connection to one's community (including the more-than-human). Though the framework outlined by Waite is focused on K-5, many of these activities can be adapted for older audiences, especially solutions for relational understanding are lacking in justice discourse."

Steve Sassaman, PhD, *CTAS: Clinical Assistant Professor and Outdoor Recreation Program Director, Arizona State University School of Community Resources and Development*

Teaching Environmental Justice in the Elementary Classroom

This timely book discusses the importance of teaching environmental justice at the elementary level and provides teachers with the tools to implement this instruction in their existing curriculum. It proves that environmental justice education isn't just a science issue—it's a human rights imperative that our students depend on.

Pulling from her personal experience as an elementary teacher and public school district STEM specialist, author Kimi Waite embraces the interdisciplinary nature of environmental justice and offers guidance on cultivating environmental justice literacy. She presents a comprehensive framework for elementary teachers to integrate equity and justice into their environmental curricula, provides entry points for implementing environmental justice into lesson planning, and offers ideas for long-term projects that students can bring outside the classroom. Additional features include real-world examples, reflection questions, supplemental resources, strategies for navigating community pushback, and practical tools you can use in your classroom.

Relevant for in-service elementary educators, administrators, and curriculum specialists alike, this book is essential reading for your lesson planning around equity in environmental education. You'll come away feeling empowered to equip your students with the knowledge and civic agency to build a truly just and sustainable future.

Kimi Waite is Assistant Professor of Child & Family Studies at California State University, Los Angeles, and serves as affiliate faculty in the Ed.D. in Educational Leadership program. She is a former elementary school teacher and a district STEM Specialist.

Equity and Social Justice in Education Series
Paul C. Gorski, Series Editor

Routledge's Equity and Social Justice in Education series is a publishing home for books that apply critical and transformative equity and social justice theories to the work of on-the-ground educators. Books in the series describe meaningful solutions to the racism, white supremacy, economic injustice, sexism, heterosexism, transphobia, ableism, neoliberalism, and other oppressive conditions that pervade schools and school districts.

Igniting Real Change for Multilingual Learners
Equity and Advocacy in Action
Carly Spina

Anti-Oppressive Universal Design for Teachers
Building Equitable Classrooms
Diana Ma

Integrating Educator Well-Being, Growth, and Evaluation
Four Foundations for Leaders
Lori Cohen and Elizabeth Denevi

Humanizing Pedagogies with Multilingual Learners
Transforming Teaching in the Content Areas
Kara Mitchell Viesca and Nancy L. Commins

From Empathy to Action
Empowering K-6 Students to Create Change
Through Reading, Writing, and Research
Chris Hass, Katie Kelly, and Lester Laminack

Promoting Equitable Math Instruction
Exploring Elementary Teachers' Stories
Monica L. Gonzalez and Alesia Mickle Moldavan

The Social and Emotional Core of Equity Leadership
A Guide for Driving Change in Schools
Gianna Cassetta

Creating Inclusive Classrooms for Muslim Students
A Practical Guide for Teachers
Noor Ali

Teaching Environmental Justice in the Elementary Classroom
Entry Points for Equity Across the K-5 Curriculum
Kimi Waite

Teaching Environmental Justice in the Elementary Classroom

Entry Points for Equity Across
the K-5 Curriculum

Kimi Waite

Taylor & Francis Group

NEW YORK AND LONDON

Designed cover image: Getty Images

First published 2026
by Routledge
605 Third Avenue, New York, NY 10158

and by Routledge
4 Park Square, Milton Park, Abingdon, Oxon, OX14 4RN

Routledge is an imprint of the Taylor & Francis Group, an informa business

© 2026 Kimi Waite

The right of Kimi Waite to be identified as author of this work has been asserted in accordance with sections 77 and 78 of the Copyright, Designs and Patents Act 1988.

All rights reserved. The purchase of this copyright material confers the right on the purchasing institution to photocopy or download pages which bear a copyright line at the bottom of the page. No other parts of this book may be reprinted or reproduced or utilised in any form or by any electronic, mechanical, or other means, now known or hereafter invented, including photocopying and recording, or in any information storage or retrieval system, without permission in writing from the publishers.

For Product Safety Concerns and Information please contact our EU representative GPSR@taylorandfrancis.com. Taylor & Francis Verlag GmbH, Kaufingerstraße 24, 80331 München, Germany.

Trademark notice: Product or corporate names may be trademarks or registered trademarks, and are used only for identification and explanation without intent to infringe.

ISBN: 978-1-041-02709-6 (pbk)
ISBN: 978-1-003-62070-9 (ebk)

DOI: 10.4324/9781003620709

Typeset in Palatino
by codeMantra

Access the Support Material: www.routledge.com/9781041027096

To all of my students: Past, present, and future.

To all of the teachers who dare to teach the truth, whether about systemic racism or environmental justice: Your bravery, tenacity, and dedication to justice are a source of hope and inspiration.

Contents

Support Material	*xi*
Acknowledgements	*xii*
Meet the Author	*xiii*
Introduction	**1**
Why Students Need You To Teach About Environmental Justice	1
How to Use This Book	4

Part 1: Getting Started—What Do I Need to Know to Teach about Environmental Justice?   **7**

1   Laying the Foundations for Teaching Environmental Justice in the K-5 Classroom   9

2   What Are Americans' Beliefs about Environmental Justice and Climate Justice?   40

Part 2: The First Steps—Shifting the Focus from Mainstream Environmentalism to Environmental Justice   **67**

3   Shifting from Mainstream Environmentalism to Environmental Justice   69

4   Towards an Intersectional Environmental Justice   91

Part 3: Implementing the First Steps—A Toolkit of Curricular Entry Points   **115**

5   A Toolkit of Initial Starting Points for Teaching Environmental Justice   117

Part 4: Digging Deeper—Geography for Environmental Justice Literacy and Action   **139**

6   Thinking Like a Geographer   141

7   GIS and Mapping for Environmental Justice   159

Conclusion   176

Appendix: List of Online Resources and Hyperlinks   *179*

Support Material

A PDF of the Appendix with clickable URLs and hyperlinks is available as Support Material on the Routledge website. To access the PDF, visit www.Routledge.com/9781041027096 and click the dropdown option that says Support Material.

Acknowledgements

Thank you to my grandfather, who taught me that my culture and history as a Japanese American are essential to being an environmentalist. Thank you to my family for always supporting my dreams and ambitions. I am grateful to Paul Gorski, editor for Routledge's Equity and Social Justice in Education series, for believing in the vision for this book. I would also like to express my gratitude to the Routledge editorial team.

Meet the Author

Kimi Waite is Assistant Professor of Child & Family Studies at California State University, Los Angeles, and serves as affiliate faculty in the Ed.D. in Educational Leadership program. A former elementary school teacher in South Los Angeles and a district STEM specialist in Compton, she has received both national and state awards for her leadership in environmental education, social studies, and climate change education. She is an early career fellow with the UCLA Center for Diverse Leadership in Science; the 2021 California Council for the Social Studies Outstanding Elementary Social Studies Teacher of the Year; a 2021 Public Voices Fellow on the Climate Crisis with the OpEd Project and the Yale Program on Climate Change Communication; and a 2019 Environmental Education 30 Under 30, awarded by the North American Association for Environmental Education. Since 2019, she has been a steering committee member for California's statewide climate change initiative, the Environmental and Climate Change Literacy Projects (ECCLPs). Her work has been published by outlets such as *PBS, The Boston Globe, Grist, Ms. Magazine, The Progressive Magazine, National Geographic's Education Blog, Rethinking Schools Magazine,* and various academic journals. She is the co-author of the book *What Teachers Want to Know About Teaching Climate Change: An Educator's Guide to Nurturing Hope and Resilience (K-12)* (Corwin Press, 2025).

Introduction

Why Students Need You to Teach about Environmental Justice

Unrelenting, extreme, and record-breaking describe the heat waves in the summers of 2024 and 2025. According to the European Union's Copernicus Climate Change Service (2024), July 22, 2024, was Earth's hottest day since at least 1940. However, while heatwaves and the Earth's rising temperatures are often seen as a "science" issue, there are wider human rights and justice implications, which means that teaching about the environment is not just the responsibility of the science teacher. Similarly, on July 25, 2024, the Secretary-General of the United Nations, António Guterres, released a "Call to Action on Extreme Heat" in response to the deadly impacts of rising temperatures worldwide (United Nations, n.d.). He specified caring for the vulnerable, protecting workers, boosting resilience using data and science, and limiting global average temperature increases to 1.5 degree Celsius. This debilitating heat is everywhere, but communities of color, lower-income populations, and other vulnerable communities disproportionately experience climate change, environmental impacts, and extreme heat. These are known as environmental injustices. In response to environmental injustices, environmental justice is the desired outcome.

Environmental justice is an interdisciplinary topic relevant to teachers of all subjects, as well as administrators, curriculum specialists, and preservice teachers. Despite this, environmental justice has historically been excluded from environmental and sustainability education efforts. A report from the

DOI: 10.4324/9781003620709-1

North American Association for Environmental Education and Edge Research (2022) found that 74% of U.S. teachers and 80% of administrators agree that climate change will have an overwhelming impact on students' futures. In addition, parents overwhelming agree that students should be taught climate change in school: More than 80% of parents in the United States support the teaching of climate change—and that support crosses political divides, according to the results of an NPR/Ipsos poll: Whether they have children or not, 66% of Republicans and 90% Democrats agree that the subject needs to be taught in school (Kamenetz, 2019). However, you cannot truly teach about the environment or even climate change without also teaching about race, justice, and equity. I can speak from personal and professional experience.

I was always fascinated by the natural world. As a small child, my most prized possessions were my "treasures" (sea glass, rocks, shells, and twigs) that I stored in recycled jam jars. In the morning and early evenings, I would always watch with awe, wonder, and pure delight as the sunlight hit the glass jars I had lined up along my bedroom windowsill. The bright light would dance across the wall in a rainbow, illuminating my wonderful treasures, making them seem even more magical. This feeling of pure awe, wonder, and delight is why I love the environment, and it is one of the many reasons I love teaching elementary students.

However, as an Asian American, I never saw myself reflected in the school curriculum. I always experienced a disconnect between my love of the environment and school, because in the curriculum, or popular culture, the people doing "environmental" things or the people who were deemed "environmentalists" were typically white, blonde children or white men. This erasure and invisibility deterred my love of science and the environment and diminished my confidence in learning about this topic. As I grew older, what I loved most about the natural world was further reduced by dry and dull lessons that involved memorizing facts in long, boring textbooks. It was not until I became a public school teacher that my passion for the environment re-energized. I rediscovered my love of the environment by seeing the wonder and awe in my kindergarten students' eyes. However, I realized that there was yet another educational disconnect, and this time, my predominantly Black and Brown students were experiencing it.

As a former kindergarten teacher in South Los Angeles, I frequently searched for—and could not find—curriculum, professional development, and books to help my students understand their lived experiences of polluted water, polluted air, extreme heat, and a lack of greenery in their neighborhoods. Additionally, as a former district STEM specialist in Compton, I have experienced days when I got headaches caused by gas leaks, and there were power outages due to extreme heat or storms. These professional and personal experiences, particularly the sharp observations by my five- and six-year-old students about the inequities in their environment, motivated me to focus on environmental education and environmental justice education as an area of research.

Now, as a higher education faculty member and an Assistant Professor who teaches undergraduates and future elementary teachers, the realities of our climate emergency are again at my doorstep. When I wrote the proposal for this book, a triple-digit heatwave was unfolding in Los Angeles. I was concerned about my students' health, comfort, and learning conditions, so I had to adapt my instruction to an online format. Unfortunately, this is an all-too-common experience for teachers and students in underfunded public schools that lack air conditioning or proper ventilation.

As I wrote the book's first and second chapters in January 2025, Los Angeles County was experiencing a major wildfire. My students, all Black, Brown, and Asian American, noticed the media cycle focusing on the loss of celebrity mansions in the Pacific Palisades and not the historically Black community in Altadena, or the traditionally working-class Latine communities in East Los Angeles who were also heavily impacted. The news cycle also focused solely on climate change, with no attention to larger root causes like systemic racism and historic redlining policies, dependence on fossil fuels, or the negligence of local public utility companies. As teachers, administrators, curriculum specialists, teacher educators, and professors, our work to teach for environmental justice cannot and should not be separated from the current socio-political moment, which the return of the Trump Administration has exacerbated. The climate emergency and the attacks on teaching true history, also known as the attacks on DEI or Critical Race Theory, are two sides of the same coin, interrelated issues. Again, you cannot truly teach about the environment or even climate change without also teaching about race, justice, and equity.

Those who attack the teaching of systemic racism and the true history of the United States want to deny our students an understanding of history and an understanding of their lived realities to uphold systems of oppression and maintain the status quo. Teaching about the connections between justice, equity, and the environment is "one of the most powerful tools we have to educate the next generation of great thinkers, civic actors, and innovators who will develop climate change mitigation and adaptation solutions. Our future depends on teaching them the truth" (Waite, 2021). As experts in multiple subjects, elementary teachers are well-equipped with the cross-curricular and interdisciplinary pedagogical skills to help students make critical and necessary connections between their lived experiences and the larger world around them. Environmental justice "especially needs to be incorporated into the social sciences, where kids are taught to be civic actors" (Waite, 2022).

However, as elementary educators, administrators, curriculum specialists, teacher educators, and professors, we must go beyond the popularized school recycling challenges, green-themed assemblies, and garden activities. While these activities serve as an initial starting point for teaching about the environment in elementary grades, they typically do not have an explicit focus on addressing justice or equity. This is a problem because our students are becoming aware of real environmental injustices and are eager to take action. Thus, it is imperative to go deeper and beyond the "green status quo" and "green business as usual." This book can help.

How to Use This Book

This book discusses the imperative of teaching environmental justice across the elementary school curriculum. The book is scaffolded for different skill levels: Part 1 introduces a history of the environmental justice movement and illustrates the relevance and importance of the book. It provides invaluable background for teachers just beginning to teach or think about environmental justice. Part 2 provides a foundation for understanding why we must shift from mainstream environmentalism to teaching and learning about environmental injustices. Part 3 provides some easy entry points in a "plug and play" style toolkit that teachers can implement into their existing curriculum. There are connections across the curriculum, which include but are not limited to: Next Generation Science Standards (NGSS), Common Core State Standards, the College, Career, and Civic Life (C3) Framework, the National Council for the Social Studies Curricular Themes, National Geography Standards, and more. The book draws upon the Learning for Justice Social Justice Standards, a framework for anti-bias education in K-12. These curricular connections give teachers entry points to teaching about environmental justice, so it is not something added to an already full plate. Part 4 delves deeper into a geography education approach and provides a rationale for why geography education is essential in teaching environmental justice. There are longer project ideas and more in-depth units of study that students and teachers can undertake in their neighborhoods to address local and global issues, including air pollution, transportation, housing equity and redlining, tree equity and urban green space, heat, and community walkability.

Many teachers might be concerned about political pushback from the community, parents, and/or administrators. To address these concerns, I discuss strategies to help teachers and students distinguish between real information and false (or intentionally misleading) content and offer real-life examples of how to engage with students, parents, and administrators who resist the teaching of environmental justice curriculum in schools. I also promote environmental justice data literacy and emphasize real environmental justice data from state and federal agencies. Students as young as kindergarten can even collect and analyze the data themselves.

Throughout the book, there is a focus on personal and professional reflection, real examples of environmental injustices in the United States and around the world, and elevating environmental justice activists, educators, and organizers who are on the ground doing the work. Finally, an appendix is provided, directing teachers to high-quality resources, a free curriculum, references for further learning, and media to utilize as classroom tools. This is the book that is needed as the culture wars and attacks on critical race theory and DEI efforts come for climate change education, particularly with the return of the Trump Administration in 2025. This is also the book I needed when I was in the classroom, and it is the book I searched for. Our students deserve to be taught the truth and equipped with the skills necessary to organize and take meaningful action for a more just and sustainable world. Join me!

References

Copernicus Climate Change Service. (2024, July 25). *A new record daily global average temperature was reached in July 2024*. Copernicus Climate Change Service. https://climate.copernicus.eu/new-record-daily-global-average-temperature-reached-july-2024?utm_source=socialmedia&utm_medium=tw&utm_id=news--record-temperature-0724

Kamenetz, A. (2019, April 22). *Most teachers don't teach climate change; 4 in 5 parents wish they did*. National Public Radio. https://www.npr.org/2019/04/22/714262267/most-teachers-dont-teach-climate-change-4-in-5-parents-wish-they-did

North American Association for Environmental Education and Edge Research. (2022, October). *The state of climate change education: Findings from a national survey of educators*. https://naaee.org/sites/default/files/2023-02/NAAEE_State%20of%20Climate%20Change%20Education%20Report_SUBMITTED%2012_12_22%5B1%5D.pdf

United Nations. (n.d.). *Secretary-General's call to action on extreme heat*. United Nations Climate Action. https://www.un.org/en/climatechange/extreme-heat

Waite, K. (2021, June 17). *Bills banning critical race theory also threaten climate education.* Grist. https://grist.org/fix/justice/teach-kids-climate-change-systemic-racism-crt/

Waite, K. (2022, August 29). *Kids need to learn about climate in every classroom, every subject.* Grist. https://grist.org/fix/opinion/climate-education-needed-in-every-classroom-every-subject/

Part 1

Getting Started—What Do I Need to Know to Teach about Environmental Justice?

Part 1 introduces a history of the environmental justice movement and illustrates the relevance and importance of the book. It provides invaluable background for teachers just beginning to teach or think about environmental justice. Part 1 introduces a history of the environmental justice movement and illustrates the relevance and importance of the book. It provides invaluable background for teachers just beginning to teach or think about environmental justice. In Chapter 1, learn from kindergarten researchers who will provide an example of how environmental justice can and should be taught in elementary classrooms, introducing the vision for this book. As educators committed to equity and justice, we will explore ways to think about disrupting the "green status quo" and "green business as usual," typically in environmental education lessons and curriculum. Learn about the Principles of Environmental Justice for K-5 Students and their corresponding elements. There are examples for classroom implementation and alignment with standards.

In Chapter 2, learn about the need to center frontline communities in the environmental justice and climate justice decision-making and solutions process. Dive further into Principle 3: In Community with Elders, Activists, and Environmental Professionals, and learn about community-centered approaches to environmental justice and climate justice. You will learn more about the American public's opinions about climate justice and how to communicate with parents and administrators effectively. For Element 1: The Ongoing Struggle for Environmental Justice, learn from second-grade water justice investigators discussing the Dakota Access Pipeline. For Element 2: Learning with/from Others, we will focus on BIPOC and LGBTQIA+ environmental justice and climate justice activists who are fighting for the education that our students deserve. At the end of both chapters, look for additional resources for teachers and students.

1

Laying the Foundations for Teaching Environmental Justice in the K-5 Classroom

Spotlight: Kindergarten Environmental Justice Researchers

This is my story. My former kindergarten students in South Los Angeles inspired my passion for teaching about the environment, particularly focusing on environmental justice and injustice. My students' inquisitive minds and their keen observations about the inequities in the environment always amazed me. However, when I searched for a curriculum, what existed at the time rarely applied to my students' lived experiences with pollution, redlining, or a lack of urban green space. Instead, most lessons and curriculum for this grade level were focused on gardening, "being green," or recycling. Having spent my career teaching in Title I schools, I also wanted to show my students that you can make a difference without all the newest "gadgets." So, I always tried to use what I already had in my classroom, or materials I found at second-hand stores, through donations, or at the dollar store. As I became more experienced in teaching, I got more comfortable with embracing my students' questions, being flexible, and embracing "teachable moments" to see where the inquiry would lead us (Waite, 2022b). Learn more in the vignette below!

The kindergarten students lined up outside the classroom door and began their morning routine of unpacking their backpacks. Jonathan and Lisa were talking about their morning walk to school.

DOI: 10.4324/9781003620709-3

Did you smell the gasoline on MLK Boulevard this morning? Pee-ewww! It was extra stinky, I felt like choking!

My five- and six-year-old kindergarten students, who are all Black and Latine, were quick to recognize the inequities related to their environment in South Los Angeles. In the morning, my students were always full of anecdotes and observations, eager to share with the class their experiences on the way to school through the neighborhood. The Sun was particularly oppressive at the beginning of the school year in mid-August, with temperatures in the high 90s.

"Ugh, it is too hot today!" *said Rosalinda, as she wiped the beads of sweat from her forehead using the back of her hand.* "I just want a huge tree to sit under," *she said.*

My students also quickly recognized that there are few green spaces in their neighborhood. A typical talking point was how schools on TV have students playing in the park. There are many trees near the school playground. My students wanted to know if other cities and neighborhoods face similar issues with a lack of gardens and trees, and why this is the case.

In true teacher fashion, I wanted to capitalize on my students' curiosity. I told the class that we should "ask the laptop."

Google Maps is an excellent tool for getting a "bird's-eye" *view of an area. The first step is to use Google Maps to locate the parks and green spaces in the community and determine their distance from the school.*

I projected Google Maps onto the whiteboard. My students were learning to read maps as part of our social studies curriculum. I showed the map's features: streets, buildings, and green space.

De'Shawn said, "I see our school!" *I motioned for him to come up to the whiteboard to show the class.*

De'Shawn said, "It is all grey up around there, there's no nature!" *(pointing to the area around the school).*

Pointing to the Google Maps projection on the whiteboard, I showed my students how to count the number of city blocks. I said, "Count the number of city blocks to the nearest park. How do I find the park? Raise your hand."

Mateo raised his hand and said, "It is the green!"

Yes, I said, "We know this is a park over here because it is green. However, I want to know more. How many blocks away from the school is the park, and how long will it take me to get there?"

The students counted in unison together: "One, two, three, four, five, six, seven, eight, nine, ten, eleven, twelve, thirteen, fourteen...." *A collective gasp filled the room.*

"Oh my gosh, that is so far," *Jaime said.*

"I wonder about those schools you see on TV," *I said.* "How close is a park to Beverly Hills schools?" "That is probably a city you see on TV."

"Like Beverly Hills Chihuahua!" said Jose.

I changed the Google Maps city to Beverly Hills and typed it into the search function. A loud collective gasp filled the room again, and students exclaimed, "Whoa, look at all that green!"

I found a school on the map and told students to count. Moises interjected and said, "Look, I see a bunch of green right there, right next to the school."

"Excellent, Moises," I said. Now, everyone, take out our scientist notebooks. Remember that we have been practicing making bar charts in math. We will create a bar chart comparing our school to the one we see in Beverly Hills.

"How many blocks away from our school is the closest park?" My students began to write in their notebooks with enthusiasm, and some pulled out their fingers to keep track of the city blocks to double-check.

"How many blocks away from this school in Beverly Hills is the closest park?" My students resumed writing in their notebooks.

I asked the class, "What is the difference between blocks?"

"THIRTEEN! THIRTEEN BLOCKS," the class shouted.

"That is nuts and not fair!" said Charlotte. "People need to know this!"

"You are right, it is not fair," I said. "In a city, who makes the decisions and is the leader? Do they need to know about this problem?"

"YEAH!" the kindergartners shouted with excitement. "That is the Mayor," said Desiree.

"Okay, excellent work, class. Yes, you are right, Desiree; we should write to the Mayor and inform them that this is a problem. That is our writing assignment today. Then we can mail the letters to the Mayor's office!"

This provides a great transition to the next multidisciplinary lesson, which will focus on civic engagement and activism for environmental justice. Students can write to the Mayor and express their concerns about the issue of a lack of green space in their city. As an extension, students can create an awareness campaign to advocate for change in their school community and at home.

As a few key takeaways from this vignette, consider the following points: The entry point to this multidisciplinary lesson was my students' observations about their environment. The entry point came from an "everyday interaction," such as morning chatter when students discuss their walk to school with friends. As the teacher, I noticed what my students were saying and observing about the environment, and then I invited their conversation into the classroom! Using their observations as a foundation, my students are rescarchers. Together, we created a lesson that allowed them to utilize real Geographical Information Systems (GIS) tools, like Google Maps, to analyze and research the inequities in their environment. Mapping allowed me to connect to social studies standards, and the class discussion achieved Common

Core speaking and listening standards. Students were then able to analyze this data using math standards, such as counting, and create bar graphs to represent the data. Students can write a city official and integrate writing standards to take it further. This vignette serves as an excellent primer for introducing environmental justice lessons in the elementary school classroom. It also shows that our elementary school students, especially young learners, are primed to notice and act upon environmental injustices and are natural researchers.

As elementary teachers, curriculum specialists, administrators, and educators, we must disrupt the green "status quo." When we think of environmental education lessons or activities done in elementary schools, some classics immediately come to mind: recycling challenges, upcycled arts and crafts projects, recycling pledges, school gardens, learning about pollinators, and Earth Day celebrations. Make no mistake, these are good activities for planting the seeds of environmental awareness. However, as educators committed to social justice and equity, it is essential to disrupt this "green business as usual" and go even further so that students can begin to grapple with larger systemic issues. The Principles of Environmental Justice for K-5 Students will help you teach about environmental justice in an accessible way. These principles also build upon best practices that you are already doing in your classroom. So consider them enhancements to your professional practice, not additional add-ons!

Principles of Environmental Justice for K-5 Students

Time to dive into the Principles of Environmental Justice for K-5 Students! (Table 1.1). Look closely at Element 1: Facilitate Crucial Conversations All Year (Table 1.1). These are best practices that you are already implementing in your classroom. However, it is imperative to establish this strong foundation all year so that students are comfortable disrupting the "green status quo" and "green business as usual."

Principle 1: Encourage Student Questions and Observations about Their Environment

Element 1: Facilitate Crucial Conversations All Year
Students must be able to bring their whole selves into observing, problem-solving, and taking action. To achieve this, our students require a classroom environment where they can feel confident and safe enough to be

Table 1.1 Principles of Environmental Justice for K-5 Students

Principle	Element
Principle 1: Encourage student questions and observations	Element 1: Facilitate crucial conversations all year Element 2: Aim to cultivate and develop a critical consciousness
Principle 2: Not just a science issue	Element 1: Engagement and entry points across the curriculum Element 2: Environmental justice has a history
Principle 3: In community with elders, activists, and environmental professionals	Element 1: The ongoing struggle for environmental justice Element 2: Learning with/from others
Principle 4: Teach across geographic perspectives	Element 1: Think like a geographer

authentic. They must know their questions, observations, and lived experiences will be seen, heard, and honored. The first thing we can do as educators is create a safe and authentic learning community for our students, starting at the beginning of the year. We will explore some tips from Facing History and Ourselves (2023) for facilitating crucial conversations. These are great ideas for morning meetings to set the tone and classroom community related to Common Core English Language Arts and Speaking and Listening content standards. Use the ideas below for whole-class sentence starters or sentence frames for partner talk. Some ideas for implementation are as follows: place sentence starters on rings for students at their desks, create sentence strips, make a classroom poster, and design laminated cards. You can also modify the sentence starters according to the students' age (Table 1.2).

After establishing the foundation for a comfortable, authentic, and safe learning environment where students can be themselves and use their voices, the next element builds upon it. To disrupt the "green status quo," students must develop a critical consciousness, particularly regarding environmental inequities.

Element 2: Aim to Cultivate and Develop a Critical Consciousness

Anyone who has spent time with a five or six-year-old knows how many questions they ask! This inquisitive questioning, sense of wonder, and awareness of right and wrong are exactly why elementary school students are ideal for learning about inequities and injustices. Providing students with the tools they need to develop and refine their critical consciousness is the cornerstone of teaching about environmental justice. Brazilian educational philosopher and scholar Paulo Freire (2018) is famous for his book, *"Pedagogy of the*

Table 1.2 Facilitating Crucial Conversations

Step	Example Conversation Starters
Affirm: Affirm and appreciate someone's willingness and openness to have a conversation	• Thank you for bringing that up. • I am happy to talk to you about that.
Acknowledge: Acknowledge what someone is saying. You can paraphrase their words and feelings to make sure that they feel seen and understood	• What I hear you saying is___. Is that correct? • It sounds like you feel_____. • From your perspective and/or lived experience_____.
Ask: Asking questions can help you understand a person's thoughts, feelings, and motivations	• What do you mean by that? I want to know more. • What life experiences have made you feel that way?
Add: Relate and offer additional information. To start, you should try to connect or empathize with what they are saying	• I have had a similar experience, and I can relate. • I can understand why you think/feel that way. • I've learned that_____.
Address and Assess: Assess the person's response and notice their body language	• What are you thinking and/or feeling now? • Can you tell me more about that?
Appreciate: Affirm their willingness to talk to you and for listening to your perspective	• Thank you for taking the time to meet me. • Thank you for hearing my perspective. • Thank you for sharing your experiences and life story.

Oppressed." He defines critical consciousness as recognizing oppressive social forces and systems that shape society and taking action against them. Notably, he emphasized the importance of cultivating transformative literacy in addition to the functional and academic literacy acquired in school. Learners should read the word and the world (Freire, 1985). Building upon this work, researchers have also analyzed the benefits and positive outcomes of developing a critical consciousness.

A team of researchers, led by El-Amin et al. (2017), found that critical consciousness is associated with higher academic achievement, higher self-esteem, and educational engagement. These findings demonstrate that when learners of all ages understand larger systemic issues that cause inequities, such as racism or sexism, they are less likely to blame themselves individually and are more likely to view and perceive themselves as resilient. Other researchers have expanded upon Freire's work, viewing critical consciousness as having three components. For example, Watts et al. (2011) establish the following as the three components of critical consciousness: (1) Social Analysis: The ability to name and analyze social, political, and economic forces that contribute towards inequality and inequity; (2) Political Agency: The belief that one can impact social and political change, and the feeling that if one wants to make a change, they are capable of doing it; (3) Social Action: The wide range of activities that individuals engage in to challenge oppressive forces.

While these three components of critical consciousness may seem lofty, even kindergartners can work toward this! To illustrate, in the vignette, the example of social analysis would be when the kindergartners began to notice the inequities in their environment related to urban green space and access to parks. As the teacher, I helped them refine their social analysis, and we discussed it as a class, and everyone began to share their ideas collaboratively. As the teacher, I also helped the kindergartners develop their political agency through our lessons based on their observations and questions. Once the kindergartners had the "language" and "data" to discuss their observations using GIS and Google Maps, as well as counting and numbers, they were eager to take action! Finally, for social action, the kindergartners can share their "reports" that compare the urban green spaces across different cities with the school community members or even city officials. Now that you learned about the first principle and elements of environmental justice for K-5 students, we will look at Principle 2!

Principle 2: Environmental Justice Is Not Just a Science Issue

Element 1: Engagement and Entry Points across the Curriculum

While environmental justice may often be "categorized" as a science issue, it is truly a multidisciplinary issue beyond just the science classroom. In fact, one of the leaders of the Environmental Justice Movement, Dr. Robert Bullard, is a sociologist, not a natural scientist! He defines environmental justice as the principle that "all people and communities are entitled to equal protection from environmental and public health laws and regulations" (Bullard, 1993). The U.S. Environmental Protection Agency (EPA) position adds that environmental justice must also include the "meaningful involvement of all people regardless of race, color, national origin or income concerning the development, implementation, and enforcement of environmental laws, regulations, and policies" (Bryant, 1995). However, historically, this has not been the reality for people of color and low-income communities, because "environmental justice is civil rights and a human rights issue" (Bullard, 2005, p.2).

Teaching and learning about environmental justice require an approach that analyzes different social and environmental systems, which necessitates an interdisciplinary approach involving all subjects. Time to look back at those kindergarten environmental justice researchers to see how truly multidisciplinary that lesson is: literacy, social studies, math, and geography, oh my! A standards table is provided below, allowing you to examine how this lesson is not only student-inquiry driven but also rich in standards alignment across the curriculum (Table 1.3).

We will continue our examination of Principle 2: Environmental Justice Is Not Just a Science Issue. After seeing how multidisciplinary a lesson on environmental justice can be, we will explore Element 2: Environmental Justice Has a History. There are numerous significant connections between social studies, geography, and environmental justice that often receive insufficient attention. By learning about the history of the Environmental Justice Movement, you will be able to find even more entry points in your existing curriculum. Below are some crucial events in the Environmental Justice Movement. Note that this section is not all-inclusive and has a U.S. focus. There will be international examples in Chapter 5. For ease of implementation in the K-5 classroom, the Civil Rights Movement (an elementary school classroom classic) is the major event and catalyst to start the timeline. Additional examples of settler colonialism are presented in the next section of this chapter.

Table 1.3 Kindergarten Environmental Justice Researchers Standards Alignment

Activity	Standards
Class discussion about students' observations	**Common Core Speaking and Listening** *CCSS.ELA-Literacy.SL.K.1* Participate in collaborative conversations with diverse partners about *kindergarten topics and texts* with peers and adults in small and larger groups. *CCSS.ELA-Literacy.SL.K.4* Describe familiar people, places, things, and events, and, with prompting and support, provide additional detail.

(Continued)

Table 1.3 (Continued)

Activity	Standards
Using Google Maps (GIS tool)	**National Council for the Social Studies Curricular Theme** *Theme 3: People, Places, and Environments*: The study of people, places, and environments enables us to understand the relationship between human populations and the physical world. **National Geography Standard** *Essential Element: The World in Spatial Terms* Geography Standard 1: How to use maps and other geographic representations, geospatial technologies, and spatial thinking to understand and communicate information
Counting city blocks and making bar graphs in a scientific notebook	**Math Common Core State Standards** *K.CC.A.1* Count to 100 by ones and by tens. *K.CC.A.3* Write numbers from 0 to 20. Represent a number of objects with a written numeral 0–20 (with 0 representing a count of no objects).

Element 2: Environmental Justice Has a History

Looking Back: A Brief History of the Environmental Justice Movement
First, I would like to start with events that provide a fresh perspective on two historical figures in the elementary school classroom: Martin Luther King Jr. and Cesar Chavez. The Memphis Sanitation Strike and the Delano Grape Strike demonstrate that these crucial men were not only civil rights leaders

but also environmental justice advocates. However, this aspect of their environmental history is often absent from schools. We are going to change that! There are also sample lesson ideas for teaching the Memphis Sanitation Strike and the Delano Grape Strike for third, fourth, and fifth graders. While written for upper elementary, teachers can modify the sample lesson plan ideas for younger grade levels.

Memphis Sanitation Strike

We know that sanitation workers collect the trash in cities, but we might not think about them often, except when we see their trucks in the early mornings. However, they play an essential role in environmental justice. What role do sanitation workers play in the Environmental Justice Movement? Time to find out! The Civil Rights Movement of the 1960s raised concerns about public health dangers, which also constitutes an environmental justice issue. On February 1, 1968, Echol Cole and Robert Walker, two Memphis garbage collectors, were crushed to death by a truck malfunction. Frustrated by the city's untimely response and a clear and established pattern of the abuse and neglect of Black employees, 1,300 Black men from the Memphis Department of Public Works went on strike on February 11, 1968. Led by garbage collector turned union organizer T.O. Jones, the strike was supported by the president of the American Federation of State, County, and Municipal Employees (AFSCME) as workers fought for better safety standards, a livable wage, and recognition of their union. The night before his assassination in April 1968, Martin Luther King Jr. told the group, "We have got to give ourselves to this struggle until the end. Nothing would be more tragic than to stop at this point in Memphis. We have got to see it through" (King, "I have been to the Mountaintop," 217). This event was the first time African Americans had mobilized a national, broad-based group in opposition to environmental injustices. Now, we will examine a sample lesson to see how this can be implemented in an elementary classroom and what it might look like.

Memphis Sanitation Strike Activity: Grades 3–5

A great way to introduce concepts in the elementary classroom and engage students around an issue is through picture books! A captivating picture book that integrates the Memphis Sanitation Strike into your classroom is *Memphis, Martin, and the Mountaintop: The Sanitation Strike of 1968* by Alice Faye Duncan. This historical fiction picture book showcases the story of a nine-year-old named Lorraine Jackson who witnessed the Memphis Sanitation Strike. Below is a sample activity for grades 3–5 with writing prompts and suggested extension activities. It can be modified for the class's needs and applies to different grade levels (Table 1.4).

Table 1.4 Teaching the Memphis Sanitation Strike

Materials, Standards, and Vocabulary	Sample Questions to Ask during the Read-Aloud	Sample Writing Prompts after Read-Aloud
Picture Book: • *Memphis, Martin, and the Mountaintop: The Sanitation Strike 1968* by Alice Faye Duncan. **Read-Along Video by Gilder Lehrman Institute:** • https://www.gilderlehrman.org/history-resources/videos/memphis-martin-and-mountaintop-sanitation-strike-1968 **Common Core Standards:** • CCSS.ELA-Literacy.RL.3.1, 3.2, & 3.3; • CCSS.ELA-Literacy.RL.4.1, 4.2, & 4.3; • CCSS.ELA-Literacy.RL.5.1, 5.2, & 5.3 **Vocabulary and Key Concepts:** • Sanitation Worker • Discrimination • Jim Crow Laws • Protest	**Environmental Justice:** • What is a sanitation worker? • What important work do sanitation workers do for the city and the people in the city? • What would happen if they went on strike? **Memphis-1968:** • What happened before sanitation workers demanded better working conditions? • How did the Memphis Mayor treat the sanitation workers? Was this justified or not? • Why did the sanitation workers go on strike? • What were the sanitation workers paid? Who benefits from keeping workers' wages low? **MLK Jr.:** • James Lawson called his friend, MLK, Jr., to come to Memphis to support the strike. Should only those involved support the strike? Why or why not? • Mamma and Daddy do not read well since they did not finish high school. Lorraine tells them about Martin Luther King Jr.'s visit to Memphis. How did they feel when they knew MLK Jr. was coming?	**Environmental Justice:** • What role do sanitation workers play in environmental justice? Use evidence from the book and/or class discussions to support your answer. **Strike:** • Is a strike an effective way to gain better working conditions? Why or why not? Use evidence from the book and/or class discussions to support your answer. **MLK Jr.:** • We have talked about MLK Jr.'s "dream." How do workers' rights factor into his dream? Use evidence from the book and/or class discussions to support your answer.

(Continued)

Table 1.4 (Continued)

Materials, Standards, and Vocabulary	Sample Questions to Ask during the Read-Aloud	Sample Writing Prompts after Read-Aloud
• Racial Segregation • Racism • Strike	• What did MLK Jr. mean when he said, "All labor has dignity?" • On April 3, 1968, MLK Jr. gave a speech called "The Mountaintop." He said, "I may not get there with you, but we as a people will make it to the promised land." What did he mean by this? • Mrs. Coretta Scott King continued the strike after MLK Jr. was killed. Why did she do this? • Did the Mayor ever bargain with the sanitation workers to end the strike? Why or why not? • At the end of the book, Lorraine says, "Freedom is never free." What does she mean by this?	

To further explore this lesson and help elevate this largely untold history, here are some extension ideas that incorporate creativity, critical thinking, 21st-century skills, and digital literacy. First, students can create their own books about the Memphis Sanitation Strike using the Book Creator app and share them with a buddy class in a different grade, donate them to the school library, or share them with the community and their families. Another idea is to make books about why labor and environmental justice play a part in Martin Luther King Jr.'s "dream." This is also a good opportunity to learn more about the sanitation workers in your city and the critical role they play in environmental justice. How much are your city sanitation workers paid?

What would happen if your city's sanitation workers went on strike? Time to learn about the Delano Grape Strike, another example of connecting labor and environmental justice.

California's Central Valley and the United Farm Workers

Agriculture probably comes to mind when you think of California's Central Valley. How about solidarity and activism? Solidarity is something else that was born in the fields. California's Central Valley has a long and rich history of environmental justice activism, cross-racial labor solidarity, and union organizing among Mexican and Asian immigrant workers. This solidarity is important because,

> *As a divide-and-conquer technique to keep wages low and diminish worker power, laborers of different ethnic and racial groups were often pitted against each other. Establishing divisions and oppositions between groups is a function of white supremacy. Solidarity and coalition building are necessary for resistance, and this solidarity was often born in the fields.*
>
> (Waite, 2023)

This solidarity began in 1903 in Oxnard, California, when a multiracial alliance of Japanese and Mexican Americans formed a union of farm workers, known as the Japanese-Mexican Labor Association. This event was "historic because it was the first time members of different racial groups aligned themselves to form a cohesive labor union" (Waite, 2023). Solidarity continued. However, the contributions of Filipinos have been mainly erased, and the connections between labor justice and environmental justice have been overlooked. Oftentimes, Dolores Huerta is rarely mentioned in lessons about Cesar Chavez. However, Larry Itliong and Philip Vera Cruz are probably never mentioned. Do your students know who Larry Itliong and Philip Vera Cruz are?

Filipino farm workers led by labor leaders Larry Itliong and Philip Vera Cruz organized the Delano Grape Strike and Boycott. On September 8, 1965, over 800 Filipino farm workers affiliated with the Agricultural Workers Organizing Committee (AWOC) went on strike at ten grape vineyards around Delano, California. Their demands were increases in their hourly rate and their piece rate (National Park Service, n.d.). Additionally, a week after the strike, the predominantly Mexican National Farm Workers led by Cesar Chavez joined them. The two groups joined to create the "United Farm Workers Union," with Cesar Chavez and Larry Itliong as the assistant directors. This strike would be known as the Delano Grape Strike of 1965 and lasted five years (Zinn Education Project, n.d.).

However, scholars Pulido and Peña (1998) inform us that environmental justice struggles in the Central Valley began as early as the 1960s, with the signing of the first United Farm Workers (UFW) Union contracts, which created worker-led health committees and contract agreements that restricted the use of pesticides like DDT. The struggles for environmental justice combined the public's concerns about dangerous pesticide exposure with farm workers' rights to better working conditions, making environmental justice a people-centered and people-focused movement. Next, learn to bring this vital information into the elementary classroom below!

Teaching the Delano Grape Strike and Farm Worker Solidarity: Grades 3–5

One of the important lessons for students is the history of cross-racial labor solidarity, specifically the union activism between Mexican and Asian immigrant workers; their struggles were interconnected. It is also essential for students to analyze and critically think about this "divide and conquer" technique used throughout history to pit marginalized groups against each other, which is a centuries-old colonial strategy. Here is another great picture book to help introduce these crucial concepts to your students. For students to learn about the contributions of Filipino farm workers, particularly about Larry Itliong, a notable picture book is *Journey for Justice: The Life of Larry Itliong*, written by Dr. Dawn Bohulano Mabalon, a prominent Filipina American historian, and Gayle Romasanta. Below is a sample activity for grades 3–5 with writing prompts and suggested extension activities. The lesson can be taught over a few days, modified for your class's needs, and adapted for different grade levels (Table 1.5).

To take this lesson further, here are some extension ideas. Students can watch the music video by Filipino artist AJ Rafael entitled "Our Friend Larry Itliong." The link is here: https://youtu.be/f5Rljoi2ArU?feature=shared. For a visual and performing arts connection, students can create music videos, plays, or skits, highlighting the environmental justice connections in Larry Itliong's story. During a back-to-school event, students can perform this music video, play, or skit for the school community or parents. Students can also consider how art can serve as a means to further activism and social justice causes, particularly in the context of environmental justice.

Next, we will learn why emphasizing geography, place, and location is essential in the Environmental Justice Movement. In particular, the proximity of toxic waste sites to schools and places of work in historically marginalized communities is a concern. Why do you think this is problematic? There is also an emphasis on law and litigation as tools to push back against and resist these injustices, and on civil disobedience, community organizing, and

Table 1.5 Teaching the Delano Grape Strike and Farm Worker Solidarity

Materials, Standards, and Vocabulary	Sample Questions to Ask during the Read-Aloud	Sample Writing Prompts after Read-Aloud
Picture Book: • *Journey for Justice: The Life of Larry Itliong* by Dawn Bohulano Mabalon, with Gayle Romasanta. **Read Aloud Video:** • https://youtu.be/4izeyu74lWQ?feature=shared **Author Interview:** • https://youtu.be/86eZPI9S8aE?feature=shared **PBS Delano Manongs:** https://www.pbs.org/video/kvie-viewfinder-delano-manongs/ **Vocabulary:** • Farm Worker • Pesticide • Solidarity • Labor Strike • Union • Boycott • Labor Activist	**Accessing Background Information:** • Show students the PBS video of the Delano Manongs and ask them what they notice about the working conditions • Show students the author interview video. Why was it essential for the author to write a book about Larry Itliong? What was the author's purpose? **Farm Workers and Labor Activism:** • What were the various agricultural industries Larry worked in? • Why do you think Filipino farm workers were paid less than the white workers? • What did the white workers do when the bosses did not give them a raise? • What lessons did Larry learn while working in different agricultural industries nationwide? • Why was society blaming the Mexican and Filipino workers for the economy? What did the United States do? • How did Larry become a leader and voice for Filipino farm workers? What is a union organizer?	**Environmental Justice:** • What are pesticides, and why do farmers use them? How could pesticides be dangerous to farmers and food consumers? Use evidence from the book and/or class discussions to support your answer. • What environmental protections should farm workers have? Use evidence from the book and/or class discussions to support your answer.

(Continued)

Table 1.5 (Continued)

Materials, Standards, and Vocabulary	Sample Questions to Ask during the Read-Aloud	Sample Writing Prompts after Read-Aloud
Common Core Standards: • Speaking & Listening CCSS.ELA-LITERACY.SL.1 • Language CCSS.ELA-LITERACY.L.4.1	• What happened at the Delano Grape Strike? What were their demands? • Why did growers start hiring Mexican workers? • What was the outcome of the Delano Grape Strike? • What does solidarity mean?	

community mobilization. Like sanitation workers and farm workers, lawyers and community members like you and your students also play an essential role in fighting for environmental justice. Check it out!

Bean v. Southwestern Waste Management

If you look at a map, how close is your school to the nearest dump or landfill? Why would having a dump or landfill near a school be problematic? What would the health implications be? How would the homeowners and community members in the neighborhood be impacted? In December 1979, in Houston, Texas, a group of Black homeowners initiated a fight to prevent the Whispering Pines Sanitary Landfill from being located within 1,500 feet of a local public school. In protest, residents formed the Northeast Community Action Group (NECAG). NECAG and its attorney, Linda McKeever Bullard, filed a class action lawsuit to block the landfill from being built. *Bean v. Southwestern Waste Management, Inc.* was the first lawsuit in the United States alleging environmental discrimination in waste facilities under civil rights laws. Although the law could not prevent the landfill construction, it was groundbreaking as it sent a clear message of environmental justice. Learn how community members' pressure, resistance, and civil disobedience have helped promote environmental justice!

Sit-In against Warren County Polychlorinated Biphenyl Landfill

Polychlorinated biphenyls (PCBs) are highly toxic and carcinogenic chemicals previously used in electrical products, paints, rubber, plastics, and pigments. PCBs are released from poorly maintained hazardous waste sites, improper disposal, and illegal or improper dumping. How would you feel if a PCB landfill or dump site were near your school? Now, how about near your own house or neighborhood? The second time African Americans mobilized a national, broad-based group in opposition to environmental injustices was a non-violent sit-in protest against a PCB landfill in Warren County, North Carolina. According to Schlosberg and Collins (2014),

> *the resistance to dumping highly toxic waste in a poor African American community brought together civil rights activists and black political leaders, along with environmentalists. It was the first significant action joining civil rights and white campaigners since the 1960s.*
>
> (p.2)

Over 500 environmentalists and civil rights activists were arrested. The protest was unsuccessful in halting construction. However, activists and scholars widely understand this event as the catalyst for the Environmental Justice Movement.

Solid Waste Sites and the Houston Black Community

By now, we can see a pattern of environmental injustice: Toxic dumpsites and landfills are in predominantly Black neighborhoods. However, how do the communities affected by these environmental injustices get city and government officials to notice and act? Here is where lawyers and scholars can help! This pattern is part of a much larger systemic issue: Environmental racism. What is it? Why does it matter to me as a teacher, administrator, or curriculum specialist? You are in the right place!

What are some examples of environmental racism that are apparent in your state, county, or city? If you cannot think of any locally, how about nationally? Robert Bullard (1983), the husband of lawyer Linda McKeever Bullard, conducted the first study documenting the location of municipal waste disposal facilities in Houston, Texas. The study, *Solid Waste Sites and the Houston Black Community*, was the first comprehensive account of environmental racism in the United States. Bullard (1983) and his researchers discovered that African American neighborhoods in Houston were chosen as sites for toxic waste dumps. Due to the 1982 Warren County sit-in, the United States General Accounting Office (1983) study provided empirical support for claims of environmental racism. The report found that three out of four hazardous waste landfills were located in communities where African Americans made up at least 26% of the population, and whose family incomes were below the poverty level. As educators, we are used to teaching our students vocabulary words. This study is essential to know because it provides the necessary language and vocabulary to describe the problem. It explicitly calls out and directly confronts the problem: It is environmental racism!

Similarly, another significant finding came from the United Church of Christ's Commission on Racial Justice (1987), which analyzed the relationship between the location of hazardous waste sites and the racial and socioeconomic composition of host communities nationwide. The study found that over 15 million African Americans, 8 million Hispanics, and half of all Asian and Pacific Islanders and Native Americans resided in communities with at least one abandoned or uncontrolled toxic waste site. These significant findings addressed race, class, and environment at the national level. Do you know where your local community's landfills or toxic waste sites are? Is it in a historically marginalized community?

Now that environmental racism has been defined and placed in its historical context, we are going to learn about coalition building in solidarity and the federal government's subsequent response to this. Do you think the federal government would respond if it were not for the pushing and persistence from the people on the ground? Ordinary people rarely get to participate in groundbreaking events that quite literally make history! It is time to learn about the First National People of Color Environmental Leadership Summit and the creation of the principles of environmental justice.

First National People of Color Environmental Leadership Summit

On October 24, 1991, the First National People of Color Environmental Leadership Summit in Washington, DC, sponsored by the United Church of Christ's Commission for Racial Justice did precisely that. They made history! At this summit, approximately 1,000 people from all 50 states, including Puerto Rico, Chile, Mexico, and the Marshall Islands, were in attendance. They formed a "think tank," described as "one of the most important events in the history of the Environmental Justice Movement" (Berndt, 2021).

At this summit, participants sought to redefine the concept of the "environment" and move beyond mainstream definitions, which often regarded the environment as a pristine natural wilderness area. This mainstream definition is problematic and removed from the lived experiences and everyday life of working people and Black, Indigenous, and People of Color (BIPOC) communities. The Environmental Justice Movement redefined the conception of the environment to be where people "lived, worked, studied, played, and prayed" (Berndt, 2021), which allowed the "environment" to address a range of interconnected issues from toxic pollution, to workers' rights and safety, to housing and transportation.

The Summit participants also created and adopted a consensus document called The 17 Principles of Environmental Justice. The Summit and the Principles outlined a process for ongoing communication, bringing environmental justice and environmental injustices to the national stage. As a result, the federal government responded, which was quite the victory! The 17 Principles of Environmental Justice will appear in Chapter 5. It might be helpful to have students consider other historical events where people have come together and established their own "rules," so to speak.

The Federal Government Responds

If you know federal environmental justice initiatives, do you know how they started? Due to the tireless pushing and advocacy work of environmental justice activists, community members, and leaders around the country! Power to the people! President George H.W. Bush Sr. established an Environmental Equity Working Group in 1992, led by EPA Administrator William Reilly. This resulted in the initiation of federally sponsored environmental justice meetings with community leaders to create solutions.

Additionally, in 1994, President Clinton issued Executive Order 12898, "Federal Actions to Address Environmental Justice in Minority Populations and Low-Income Populations." The executive order directed the federal government to integrate environmental justice into its decision-making process. Why do you think it is important to have environmental justice at the federal level and in federal policies and legislation?

It called into focus the environmental conditions and health experienced by low-income, minority, and tribal populations (U.S. Department of Energy, n.d.). It called for achieving environmental justice and promoting nondiscriminatory programs that impact the environment and human health. This Order required federal agencies to make environmental justice an integral part of their missions and to establish an environmental justice strategy. An Interagency Working Group on Environmental Justice (EJIWG) was created, and you can learn more about federal environmental justice activities by exploring the Agency Environmental Implementation Progress Reports. Your students can also research these groups if they are familiar with the federal government in their social studies standards and lessons. Since the Trump Administration prioritized slashing environmental justice efforts due to its "anti-DEI" campaigns, the federal agencies listed below all previously had websites dedicated to their environmental justice strategies. When I checked in April 2025, the websites for the environmental justice strategies for each federal agency were removed, and I had to remove the corresponding website links from the list below:

- Environmental Protection Agency (EPA)
- Department of Commerce (DOC)
- Department of Agriculture (USDA)

- Department of Defense (DoD)
- Department of Energy (DoE)
- Department of Education (DofEd)
- Department of Health and Human Services
- Department of Housing and Urban Development (HUD)
- Department of Homeland Security (DHS)
- Department of Justice (DOJ)
- Department of the Interior (DOI)
- Department of Labor (DOL)
- Department of Veterans Affairs (VA)
- Department of Transportation (DOT)
- General Services Administration (GSA)
- Small Business Administration (SBA)
- White House Offices (Biden Administration).

Threats to Environmental Justice

When writing this book, the Trump Administration had returned to the White House. As seen above, where environmental justice efforts at the federal level were drastically reduced, some questions that we, as educators committed to equity and social justice, must consider are: How will a change in the Presidential Administration impact federal environmental protections? How are federal diversity initiatives ultimately connected to environmental justice? To what extent does a Presidential Administration impact federal environmental protections? How might this affect the role of environmental protection at the state level? The Trump Administration and its allies are adamantly anti-science, anti-diversity, equity, and inclusion (DEI), and anti-human rights, which is a particularly serious combination! We recognize that threats to science, DEI, and human rights are also threats to teaching about environmental justice. As I have said, "bills banning critical race theory also threaten climate education" (Waite, 2021a). We will dive into this later in the book.

Right Now: Struggles for Environmental Justice

Principle 3: In Community with Elders, Activists, and Environmental Professionals

Element 1: The Ongoing Struggle for Environmental Justice
One of the notable events in the Environmental Justice Movement is the Dakota Access Pipeline (DAPL) protests. Have you seen images of protests on the news? While we may think of this as a one-time occurrence that happened

at a specific point, it is not a singular, isolated event in recent history. Indigenous peoples have been resisting settler colonialism for centuries, particularly in the continuing struggle for water justice and water rights. What is settler colonialism? What does this have to do with environmental justice? The goal of settler colonialism is the removal and erasure of Indigenous peoples to take and use land indefinitely and to establish property rights over land and resources. Settler colonialism is not just something horrendous from the past, but still exists today as an ongoing structure of systemic oppression that seeks to control resources, land, space, and people (Waite, 2022a).

Environmental Justice and Water Protectors
Access to clean, potable, safe, and affordable water is likely a privilege we often overlook. It is not just a concern of countries in the Global South, but it still occurs today in what we now call the United States of America. Also, according to the National Association for the Advancement of Colored People (NAACP), clean water is a major public health issue with "significant implications for community well-being, economic stability, and social justice" (NAACP, n.d.). Do you know the Native land that you are on? If you are unsure or would like to learn more, a great resource is available at https://native-land.ca/.

Do you also know your closest watershed? Where is the primary water source for your city or state? The Standing Rock Sioux Tribe in North Dakota and South Dakota relies on Lake Oahe, a reservoir of over 200 miles along the Missouri River, as the primary water source for the Standing Rock Sioux Tribe. For almost a decade, the DAPL has ignited controversy and national conversations about the unjust treatment of Indigenous people in the United States. While Indigenous struggles and resistance against settler colonialism are not new, the controversy with DAPL began escalating in 2016 when the first permits for construction were received and approved by the U.S. Army Corps of Engineers. DALP is a 1,172-mile-long underground pipeline owned by Energy Transfer Partners (ETO) that transports crude oil from North Dakota's Bakken region to an oil terminal in Patoka, Illinois. In Illinois, it connects with the Energy Transfer Crude Oil Pipeline, which brings oil to Gulf Coast refineries. Combined, these two pipelines make up the Bakken Pipeline. The most controversial and disputed section of the DAPL is the cross upstream of the Standing Rock reservation under Lake Oahe, a part of the reservoir section of the Missouri River. A leak or spill along this route would be detrimental and contaminate the reservation's cultural sites and water supply.

Large-scale grassroots protests spread the message that the proposed oil pipeline was threatening the Standing Rock Sioux tribe in North Dakota.

Thanks to far-reaching media coverage of the seven-month-long protest at Standing Rock, as well as advocacy efforts from high-profile celebrities and emerging politicians, Indigenous-led viral social media campaigns like #NoDAPL, and the police's violent response to the protestors, DAPL was kept in the spotlight and in the national consciousness after the pipeline was operational in 2017. DAPL is yet another example of how the U.S. government has exploited Indigenous peoples over centuries and intersects with the reservation's current and modern-day boundaries. To implement some of these larger ideas, a multidisciplinary lesson plan for teaching about environmental justice and water protectors can be modified for different grade levels. As seen in Table 1.6, additional curricular resources will be introduced throughout the book, particularly in Chapter 5.

Key Takeaways

Kyle Whyte (2016), a scholar of Indigenous studies and environmental justice notes, "Indigenous communities are among the first climate refugees, having to decide to relocate due to sea-level rise in the Arctic and the Gulf of Mexico, as well as other places across the U.S. sphere" (para. 8). Thus, stopping DALP and also learning about the history of settler colonialism and "land grabs," is about stopping colonialism and continued environmental harm upon Indigenous communities. As teachers committed to social justice and equity, it is essential to remember that efforts to prevent DAPL are not a single isolated event, but exist within a larger movement of Indigenous resistance. One of the ways Indigenous Nations have engaged in resistance is by documenting U.S. treaty violations over time. This requires tremendous knowledge of history, the ability to analyze and understand primary source documents from U.S. treaties, and an understanding of current struggles that violate these treaties. This is important for students because it provides a real-life lesson in using history and social studies as tools for activism and resistance. Students can even join in on compiling an "offenders" list.

For example, the Lummi have been documenting U.S. treaty violations and negligence in destroying their salmon habitats, which Indigenous Nations depend on for their treaty-protected fishing rights. The Lummi Nation has tried to block the establishment of a railway and coal shipment terminal near its protected area of Xwe'chi'eXen in Washington state. Students can research the vital work that the Lummi Nation is doing, and even join in on researching and documenting other U.S. Treaty violations throughout history. As you can imagine, there are many violations! It is also crucial for students to understand that when they learn about environmental justice, they are part of a community with elders, activists, and environmental professionals. These individuals,

Table 1.6 Teaching about Water Protectors and Environmental Justice

Picture Book	*We Are Water Protectors* by Carole Lindstrom, Illustrated by Michaela Goade
Activity Kit	"We Are Water Protectors" activity kit from Roaring Brook Press: https://static.macmillan.com/static/macmillan/2020-online-resources/downloads/we-are-water-protectors-activity-kit.pdf
Illustrator Interview	Interview with Michaela Goade: https://www.youtube.com/watch?v=JvT5hsvUc2E&t=
Example Reflection Questions for Students (Can be Modified for Grade Level)	• Why is water essential? What do we use it for? • Where does our community's water come from? • How do chemicals and oils enter our waterways? • What does the "black snake" represent? • Why were the Standing Rock Sioux Tribe and others protesting the Dakota Access Pipeline? • What would you do if a pipeline were built in your community? • Where are the watersheds in our community? • What do we notice about Michaela Goade's illustrations?

Curricular Standards Connections	• **Common Core English Language Arts Speaking and Listening:** https://www.thecorestandards.org/ELA-Literacy/SL/
	• **National Council for the Social Studies Curricular Themes:** https://www.socialstudies.org/national-curriculum-standards-social-studies-chapter-2-themes-social-studies
	  → Theme 3: People, Places, and Environments;
	  → Theme 6: Power, Authority, Governance;
	  → Theme 8: Science, Technology, and Society.
	• **National Geography Standards:** https://education.nationalgeographic.org/resource/national-geography-standards-index/
	  → Geography Standard 14: How Human Actions Modify the Physical Environment
	• **National Arts Standards:** https://www.nationalartsstandards.org/
	  → Responding: Anchor Standard 8

particularly Indigenous Nations, have long defended their water, land, culture, livelihood, and lives. Now, look at Element 2: Learning with/from Others.

Element 2: Learning with/from Others

When adults and children work together, it can have a powerful impact on the world. Educational researchers Esteban Diaz and Barbara Flores (2001) believed that, in addition to a formal academic role, teachers are a "sociocultural mediator." This means that teachers, especially teachers with students from marginalized backgrounds, should be aware that children bring a wealth of personal, community, and cultural knowledge with them into the classroom. Teaching and learning become a collaborative endeavor between teachers and students, in which the teacher views the students as possessing knowledge and not just as passive recipients of knowledge. This is similar to Paulo Freire's premise of collaboration and the co-construction of knowledge. I have applied these concepts to my work in creating and facilitating partnerships between scientists, teachers, and young children, particularly around how we teach and learn about environmental issues (Waite, 2019a, 2019b, 2021b; Waite & Burgin, 2023, 2025).

I am passionate about teaching and learning about multidisciplinary environmental issues in kindergarten classrooms, particularly in partnership with scientists and STEM professionals! In this collaborative environmental learning space, students are "experts" who can help the scientists with their work. They can help by finding creative and innovative solutions, designing new prototypes to assist the scientists, and also helping the scientists rediscover a renewed sense of joy, wonder, and excitement. In the Environmental Justice Movement, there are many leaders and activists that students today may not be familiar with. That needs to change because intergenerational learning and collaboration are essential to sustaining and continuing the work of environmental justice and environmental justice education.

In this book, we will learn/from leaders in the Environmental Justice Movement, elders, youth activists, and environmental professionals. In this work, I will draw upon a three-step framework for working with STEM professionals that my colleague and I developed and subsequently tested in elementary school classrooms across North America (Waite & Burgin, 2023), entitled "Collaborative Partnerships Between Young Learners and Scientists." The steps outlined below have been adapted and are referred to as "Collaborations with Environmental Justice Elders, Activists, and Environmental Professionals." We will begin to apply these specific steps in Chapter 2!

- **Step 1: Meet the environmental professional and learn their story.**
  You can meet the professional virtually through the media or on their

website. Build a relationship through literature, learn about their mission/work, and represent the mission with an artifact they use.
- **Step 2: Join the mission.** After young learners have background knowledge of the professionals and their mission/work, they will mimic their work using age-appropriate tools. Students will collect data and use tools like professionals.
- **Step 3: Extend the mission and take civic action.** Once young learners have built the professional skill set in step two, the students will synthesize that skill into their mission to take civic action. It can expand on the work that the professional is already doing, or the young learner can take on a new mission inspired by the work of the professional, and what the student is passionate about.

Principle 4: Teach across Geographic Perspectives

When you think of "geography," maps, landforms, globes, and facts probably come to mind. However, geography is more than that. Geography is also much cooler than that! Geography studies places and the relationships between people and their environments. A geographer studies where things are, why they exist, and how they develop and change over time. There are two main branches of geography: Physical geography and human geography. Those maps and landforms you typically associate with geography are part of physical geography, the study of the world's physical features, which includes landforms, plants, soils, and bodies of water.

On the other hand, human geography studies the world's geographic features, like people, landscapes, and communities. Human geographers are primarily concerned with the cultural, economic, political, historical, technological, and social systems that shape human interactions. Human geographers also study the intersections of the human and natural worlds, which is crucial when teaching and learning about environmental justice!

Element 1: Think Like a Geographer

This book will focus on human geography, specifically how geographers wear "glasses" and look at topics, regions, and issues from various scales and perspectives. Examining these different scales and perspectives, as well as the intersections between them, enables geographers to identify patterns of interaction (Zhao et al., 2020). Here is a graphic to help you understand how human geographers think and how they look at the (Figure 1.1):

Now, let us try on the "Geographer's Glasses" for water as an environmental justice issue (Figure 1.1). If you or your students put on these glasses, the spatial perspectives would be on your right (spatial, cultural, political, etc.), and the scales would be on your left (global, regional, and local). Like going

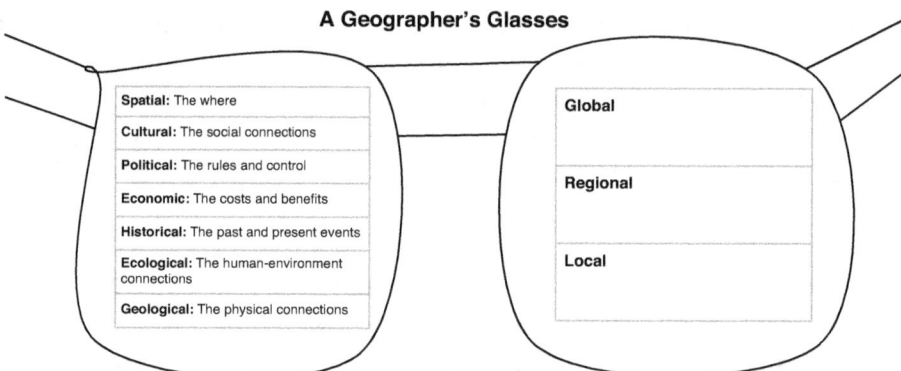

Figure 1.1 A Geographer's Glasses.

to the eye doctor's office, we will partially cover our left eye so that the only scale we can see through is local. Now is the time to take a look at water and develop some questions that students might use for projects or investigations about their local water systems, and any corresponding inequities that exist:

1   **Spatial: The "where"**
    – Where is our local water source?
    – Where is water cleaned and stored in our community?
    – Where are our school's water fountains?

2   **Cultural: The "social"**
    – What do we use water for?
    – Why is water important to people?
    – How do we use water in public places?

3   **Political: The "rules"**
    – Who controls the price of our water bills?
    – Who treats water so we can drink it?
    – Who has access to safe and clean drinking water?

4   **Economic: The "costs and benefits"**
    – Why do people buy single-use plastic bottles?
    – What problems do single-use plastic bottles cause?
    – How much money do reusable water bottles save?

5   **Historical: The "past events"**
    – How did people carry water before plastic bottles and reusable bottles?

- When were plastic bottles and reusable bottles invented?
- What do you know about Nestlé and the Morongo Tribe? Can you think of and/or research similar situations?

6 **Ecological: The "human-environmental connections"**
- How safe is tap water to drink?
- Does this vary in different communities?
- Can people own water? Should they?

You can have students wear these "glasses" and switch out which individual lenses you want students to examine an issue with. For younger students, this can take a "play-based" approach with actual glasses they can wear on their faces or draw. Students can use note cards or drawings to represent the "different lenses" on each side of the glasses, corresponding to the particular environmental justice issue being examined or discussed. A great art integration would be to have students make posters, drawings, paintings of their "glasses," or even self-portraits of themselves wearing their glasses. The number of lenses per scale and perspectives worn in the glasses can also vary by age and grade level.

Now that you have met the kindergarten environmental justice researchers and have learned about the Principles and Elements of Environmental Justice for K-5 Students, you are ready to continue your learning journey in Chapter 2! In Chapter 2, get ready to learn about the need to center frontline communities in the environmental justice and climate justice decision-making and solutions process. You will see a spotlight lesson from a second-grade class about the Standing Rock Sioux Tribe and the DAPL. There will also be an emphasis on Principle 3, and you will have the opportunity to learn from and with BIPOC and LGBTQIA+ environmental justice and climate justice activists who are fighting for the education our students deserve. Before you move on to Chapter 2, here are some reflection questions for your professional practice. Below are resources for teachers and students that relate to the content covered in Chapter 1.

Reflection Questions for Professional Practice

Chapter 1 Questions

- What are some of your best practices for centering community and student voice in your classroom? What other best practices are you

currently using to facilitate discussions about complex topics in your classroom?
- What environmental or climate injustices are happening in your state? In your local community?
- What environmental justice community organizations do you know of in your region, state, or local community? What initial ideas do you have for integrating their resources into the classroom?
- Do you teach the UN Sustainable Development Goals? If so, what UN Sustainable Development Goals can you use to teach about environmental injustices?
- What initial cross-curricular ideas do you have for teaching about environmental justice? Additional resources and ideas can be found in Chapter 5.
- Look in your classroom library. Do you have any books to teach about environmental justice? Chapter 5 provides more resources and ideas.

 Further Reading: Resources for Teachers and Students

Videos for Teachers

Facing History and Ourselves. *Schooling for critical consciousness: A conversation with Scott Seider and Daren Graves.* https://www.facinghistory.org/learning-events/schooling-critical-consciousness-conversation-scott-seider-daren-graves

Grist. *Environmental justice, explained.* https://www.youtube.com/watch?v=dREtXUij6_c

PBS. *Robert Bullard: How environmental racism shapes the U.S.* https://www.pbs.org/video/what-environmental-racism-robert-bullard-explains-yszys6/

Vogue. *Stories from Standing Rock.* https://www.youtube.com/watch?v=QFjnudxcfv0

Books for Teachers

Bullard, R. D. (Ed.). (2005). *The quest for environmental justice: Human rights and the politics of pollution* (Vol. 19, pp. 32–33). San Francisco, CA: Sierra Club Books.

Estes, N. (2024). *Our history is the future: Standing Rock versus the Dakota Access Pipeline, and the long tradition of Indigenous resistance.* Chicago, IL: Haymarket Books.

Gilio-Whitaker, D. (2019). *As long as grass grows: The Indigenous fight for environmental justice, from colonization to Standing Rock.* Boston, MA: Beacon Press.

Johnson, A. E., & Wilkinson, K. K. (Eds.). (2021). *All we can save: Truth, courage, and solutions for the climate crisis.* London: OneWorld Publications.

Méndez, M. (2020). *Climate change from the streets: How conflict and collaboration strengthen the environmental justice movement.* New Haven, CT: Yale University Press.

Seider, S., & Graves, D. (2020). *Schooling for critical consciousness: Engaging Black and Latinx youth in analyzing, navigating, and challenging racial injustice.* Cambridge, MA: Harvard Education Press.

Todrys, K. W. (2021). *Black Snake: Standing Rock, the Dakota Access Pipeline, and environmental justice.* Lincoln, NE: University of Nebraska Press.

Picture Books for Students

Hillery, T. (2020). *Harlem grown: How one big idea transformed a neighborhood.* New York, NY: Simon and Schuster.

King, H. K. (2021). *Saving American Beach: The biography of African American environmentalist MaVynee Betsch.* New York, NY: Penguin Young Readers.

Lindstrom, C. (2020). *We are water protectors.* New York, NY: Roaring Brook Press.

Mabalon, D. H. & Romasanta, G. (2018). *Journey for justice: The life of Larry Itliong.* Stockton, CA: Bridge and Delta Publishing.

Tutor, A. (2019). *Young native activist: Growing up in Native American Rights Movements.* Eaglespeaker Publishing. Independent Publishing.

Tutor, A. & Tutor, K. (2018). *Young water protectors: A story about Standing Rock (young native boy series).* Scotts Valley, CA: CreateSpace Independent Publishing.

References

Berndt, B. (2021, March 25). *30th anniversary: The first national people of color environmental leadership summit.* United Church of Christ. https://www.ucc.org/30th-anniversary-the-first-national-people-of-color-environmental-leadership-summit/

Bullard, R. D. (1983). Solid waste sites and the black Houston community. *Sociological Inquiry, 53*(2–3), 273–288.

Bullard, R. D. (1993). The legacy of American apartheid and environmental racism. *John's Journal of Legal Commentary, 9,* 445.

Bullard, R. D. (Ed.). (2005). *The quest for environmental justice: Human rights and the politics of pollution* (Vol. 19, pp. 32–33). San Francisco, CA: Sierra Club Books.

Diaz, E., & Flores, B. (2001). Teacher as sociocultural, sociohistorical mediator: Teaching to the potential. In *The best for our children: Critical perspectives on literacy for Latino students* (pp. 29–47). Teacehrs College Press.

El-Amin, A., Seider, S., Graves, D., Tamerat, J., Clark, S., Soutter, M., ..., & Malhotra, S. (2017). Critical consciousness: A key to student achievement. *Phi Delta Kappan, 98*(5), 18–23.

Facing History and Ourselves. (2023, September 26). *Straight A's for facilitating crucial conversations*. Facing History and Ourselves. https://www.facinghistory.org/resource-library/straight-facilitating-crucial-conversations

Freire, P. (1985). Reading the world and reading the word: An interview with Paulo Freire. *Language Arts, 62*(1), 15–21.

Freire, P. (2018). *Pedagogy of the oppressed: 50th Anniversary edition*. Bloomsbury Academic.

King, M. L. Jr. (1968, April 3). "I've been to the mountaintop," address delivered at Bishop Charles Mason Temple. https://archives.ubalt.edu/bsr/articles/king%20speech.pdf

NAACP. (n.d.). *Environmental & climate justice issue brief: Clean water*. https://naacp.org/resources/environmental-climate-justice-issue-brief-clean-water

National Park Service. (n.d.). *Workers united: The Delano Grape Strike and Boycott*. https://www.nps.gov/articles/000/workers-united-the-delano-grape-strike-and-boycott.htm#:~:text=On%20September%208%2C%201965%2C%20over,each%20box%20of%20grapes%20packed).

Pulido, L., & Peña, D. (1998). Environmentalism and positionality: The early pesticide campaign of the United Farm Workers' Organizing Committee, 1965–71. *Race, Gender & Class, 6*(1), 33–50. https://www.jstor.org/stable/41658847

Schlosberg, D., & Collins, L. B. (2014). From environmental to climate justice: Climate change and the discourse of environmental justice. *Wiley Interdisciplinary Reviews: Climate Change, 5*(3), 359–374. https://doi.org/10.1002/wcc.275

United Church of Christ Commission for Racial Justice. (1987). *Toxic wastes and race in the United States: A national report on the racial and socio-economic characteristics of communities with hazardous waste sites*. https://www.nrc.gov/docs/ML1310/ML13109A339.pdf

United States Department of Energy. (n.d). *Environmental justice history*. https://www.energy.gov/lm/environmental-justice-history

United States General Accounting Office. (1983). *Siting of hazardous waste landfills and their correlation with the racial and economic status of surrounding communities*. https://archive.gao.gov/d48t13/121648.pdf

Waite, K. (2019a, August 23). Strategy share: Empowering students through connections with explorers. *National Geographic Society Education Blog*.

https://blog.education.nationalgeographic.org/2019/08/23/strategy-share-empowering-students-through-connections-with-explorers/

Waite, K. (2019b, June 12) Strategy share: Environmental literacy and connections with STEM Californians. *National Geographic Society Education Blog.* https://blog.education.nationalgeographic.org/2019/06/12/strategy-share-environmental-literacy-and-connections-with-stem-californians/

Waite, K. (2021a). Bills banning critical race theory also threaten climate education. *Grist.* https://grist.org/fix/justice/teach-kids-climate-change-systemic-racism-crt/

Waite, K. (2021b). Kindergarten deforestation experts: Interdisciplinary learning for understanding and addressing global issues. *International Journal of Early Childhood Environmental Education, 8*(3), 20–39.

Waite, K. (2022a, July 25). Discussion guide–Manzanar, diverted: Tools for facilitation. *American Documentary & the Center for Asian American Media.* https://www.amdoc.org/engage/resources/manzanar-diverted-tools-facilitation/you-begin-tips-tools-facilitators/

Waite, K. (2022b, May 1). Action research for environmental justice in the kindergarten classroom. *Rethinking Schools Magazine.* https://rethinkingschools.org/articles/action-research-for-environmental-justice-in-the-kindergarten-classroom/

Waite, K. (2023, August 30). The history of Asian American labor activism is essential for today's students. *Ms. Magazine.* https://msmagazine.com/2023/08/30/asian-american-labor-women-workers/

Waite, K., & Burgin, J. (2023). Interdisciplinary learning partnerships between TK–2 students and scientists for environmental civic learning. *Social Studies and the Young Learner, 36*(1), 20–26.

Waite, K., & Burgin, J. (2025). Joyful STEAM Civics: Interdisciplinary learning collaborations between TK-2 students and scientists. *Social Studies and the Young Learner, 38*(1), 11–16.

Watts, R. J., Diemer, M. A., & Voight, A. M. (2011). Critical consciousness: Current status and future directions. *New Directions for Child and Adolescent Development, 2011*(134), 43–57. https://doi.org/10.1002/cd.310

Whyte, K. (2016, September 16). *Why the Native American pipeline resistance in North Dakota is about climate justice.* The Conversation. https://theconversation.com/why-the-native-american-pipeline-resistance-in-north-dakota-is-about-climate-justice-64714

Zhao, J., Simpson, M., Wallgrün, J. O., et al. (2020). Exploring the effects of geographic scale on spatial learning. *Cognitive Research, 5,* 14. https://doi.org/10.1186/s41235-020-00214-9

Zinn Education Project. (n.d.). (*Sept. 8, 1965). The Delano Grape Strike Began.* https://www.zinnedproject.org/news/tdih/delano-grape-strike/

2

What Are Americans' Beliefs about Environmental Justice and Climate Justice?

Spotlight: Second-Grade Water Justice Investigators

The second-grade students lined up on the hot blacktop after the recess bell rang, and many of them were still sweating and panting from the late spring sun. When Mr. Gomez rounded the corner to get his students from the blacktop, he said,

> *I hope everyone had a good recess. Remember, it's essential to stay hydrated when it's hot outside. Please make sure to finish your drinks before we get back to class. Okay, Timmy, go ahead, you can start the walk back to class.*

Timmy, the line leader, began to walk back to the classroom, and the line followed behind him like a long tail. Students began to quickly guzzle the rest of the water from their bottles as they walked down the corridor.

When the line stopped outside the classroom, Mr. Gomez said, "Okay, students, remember to put your water bottles in your backpacks or outside by the door. We do not want any spills inside the classroom." Mr. Gomez propped open the door and watched the students file inside. They looked wilted and sticky due to the heat.

"Luis, can you please turn on the air conditioning? It is very stuffy inside the classroom," said Mr. Gomez.

When the students were at their desks, Mr. Gomez said, "I am glad you're all staying hydrated. That is a good transition into our topic for today. I know a lot of you have water bottles, but do you know where the water in our community comes from?"

"I know, the duck!" said Mark. The class erupted in loud laughter.

DOI: 10.4324/9781003620709-4

"Okay, settle down, everyone!" said Mr. Gomez. "Mark, do you mean aqueduct?" he said.

"Yeah," said Mark, who grinned widely. "That long tunnel thing that we learned about in social studies. The Colorado River and Los Angeles River."

"Excellent, Mark," said Mr. Gomez. "I am so glad that you remembered. Can anyone else add on to what Mark said?"

"Mr. Gomez, he means the Colorado River Aqueduct and the Los Angeles Aqueduct," said Josephina.

"Great, yes, Josephina, that is correct," said Mr. Gomez, who pulled down from the wall a large California state map.

"We learned that the Colorado River Aqueduct is a water conveyance system that transports water to Southern California from the Colorado River." He pointed to the map.

"The Los Angeles Aqueduct is another conveyance system that transports water from the Owens Valley and the Mono Basin."

Mr. Gomez continued,

> Now that we have reviewed where our water supply comes from, I want you to talk to your table group about how chemicals and oils might get into our waterways and what you would do if that happened. Please remember to follow our class rules for respectful conversations, and you can also use the sentence frames at your desks. I will give you three minutes,

he said.

Students turn to their table groups, and a buzz of chatter quickly fills the classroom. Mr. Gomez circles the room and listens to the students' conversations.

Nodding in agreement when walking by several tables, Mr. Gomez brings the class back to attention.

"Okay, class, I heard a lot of really great ideas! I hear some common themes here, and we should discuss this together. Can I have a representative from each group share an idea?"

Dwyane raised his hand. "Mr. Gomez, we said some companies might dump the chemicals in the water because they do not want to clean them up from the factory, and it is easier to dump them."

"An excellent point!" said Mr. Gomez.

Leyla raised her hand. "Mr. Gomez, we think that people will protest if there are too many chemicals in the water."

"Excellent ideas, everyone," said Mr. Gomez. That is precisely what is happening. Today, we are going to learn more about the Standing Rock Sioux Tribe and other activists who are protesting something called the Dakota Access Pipeline (DAPL).

Our essential question is: Why are people protesting the DAPL? Let us take out our notebooks and start our writing lesson for today.

This provides a great transition to an interdisciplinary lesson on the DAPL, focusing on writing. Explore these lesson plan ideas from KQED: https://cdn.kqed.org/wp-content/uploads/sites/26/2016/12/Standing-Rock-lesson-plan.pdf.

After learning from these second-grade water justice investigators, let us consider some key points and takeaways. The teacher used an "everyday interaction" to kick off this lesson: He noticed students quickly chugging water from their water bottles after recess, which led to posing the question, "Do you know where the water in our community comes from?" This allowed students to connect to their local water supply system, review content, and activate prior knowledge previously taught during a social studies lesson. Mr. Gomez also used the best practice of "table groups" or "think-pair-share," which provided a safe space for students to explore their ideas with peers before he brought the discussion to the whole class. This provides scaffolding and support for students who are introverted and for English Language Learners. Additionally, through this practice, the teacher was addressing Principle 1: Encourage Student Questions and Observations, as well as Element 1: Facilitate Crucial Conversations All Year.

Mr. Gomez then had students ponder this problem: How do chemicals and oils get into our waterways, and what would you do if that happened? This question prompts students to consider the source of pollution and activates their curiosity and empathy by having them make a personal connection. This is a great way to segue into a larger interdisciplinary lesson on the DAPL protests. Next, the teacher can utilize the interdisciplinary lesson plan about the DAPL from KQED, which focuses not only on writing but also has connections to literacy and social studies. The lesson has vocabulary words, a video from an investigative journalism report, appropriate "stop and discuss" points during the video, discussion questions, Common Core standards connections, and recommendations of primary source documents to explore. This lesson plan would address Principle 3: In Community with Elders, Activists, and Environmental Professionals. Time to dig deeper into Principle 3 now and the corresponding elements.

The Need to Center Frontline Communities in Decision-Making and Solutions

In Chapter 1, we learned about Principle 3: In Community with Elders, Activists, and Environmental Professionals. Time to look at Element 2: Learning with/from Others. Another leader in the Environmental Justice Movement is Dr. Beverly Wright, a sociologist. Dr. Wright grew up in a highly polluted corridor in Louisiana called "Cancer Alley," which provided a catalyst for her work, studies, and leadership. Cancer Alley is known as a "sacrifice zone," which is defined as "fenceline communities of low-income and people of color, or 'hot spots' of chemical pollution where residents live immediately adjacent to heavily polluted industries or military bases" (Bullard, 2011, para 2). This is part of a larger pattern of unequal protection, constituting environmental racism.

As we also learned in Chapter 1, environmental racism was challenged in courts in a 1979 lawsuit, *Bean v. Southwestern Waste Management*. It was the first lawsuit to utilize civil rights law in challenging environmental racism. To note, it has been found that "one of the most important indicators of an individual's health is one's ZIP code" (Bullard, 2011, para. 6). To learn more about Dr. Wright and her story, in the spirit of intergenerational learning and collaboration, let us apply the "3 Steps For Working with Environmental Justice Elders, Activists, and Environmental Professionals." Take a deeper look below!

Step 1: Meet the Environmental Professional and Learn about Their Story

> Meet them virtually through the media or by viewing their website. Build a relationship through literature, see what their mission/work is about, and represent the mission with an artifact that they use in their work.

For Step 1, students can learn about Dr. Wright's work and mission by watching this brief video here: https://youtu.be/hiWj9CgXaXQ?feature=shared. Since geography, location, and place are all critical components in the Environmental Justice Movement, next, students will learn more about Cancer Alley to understand how this inspired Dr. Wright's work. For starters, why do you think it is called Cancer Alley? According to a Human Rights Watch (2024) report, for decades, the state of Louisiana, specifically the Louisiana Department of Environmental Quality (LDSE), has repeatedly failed to address the harms and detrimental effects of petrochemical operations, has been unable to enforce the federal government's minimum standards, and has also failed to protect environmental and human health.

Cancer Alley is an 85-mile stretch along the banks of the Mississippi River, between Baton Rouge and New Orleans, where communities live side by side with over 200 fossil fuel and petrochemical operations. It is reportedly the largest concentration of such plants in the Western Hemisphere (Human Rights Watch, 2024, para. 2)! Parts of Cancer Alley have the highest risk of cancer from industrial air pollution in the United States, with Black residents disproportionately impacted. However, the community has resisted, and Dr. Wright has been a key player in this resistance. When completing her studies in sociology, she noticed that the absence of community input from solutions and the solution-making process exacerbates the effects of pollution. As the founder and executive director of the Deep South Center for Environmental Justice, Wright developed the "communiversity model," which outlines a theory of change involving partnerships between universities and local communities, with an emphasis on Louisiana and other Gulf states. Speaking about the communiversity model, Wright says:

> *Developing this approach, which we call communiversity, led to many, many successes and unbelievable trust among communities. It helped to grow the environmental justice movement, being the backbone for the research and support needed to make policy changes.*
>
> (Deen, 2021, para. 5)

This example demonstrates to students how solutions to environmental justice require community-based approaches from people living in the communities themselves, rather than top-down approaches from outside organizations. What forms of community knowledge might your students have? The Deep South Center for Environmental Justice utilizes Wright's model to address and understand the challenges frontline communities experience with environmental racism, climate change, and environmental injustices. Her model also enables the Center to offer community training and education workshops, with a specific emphasis on the Gulf states. For a resource guide of the Deep South Center for Environmental Justice's programs, refer to Table 2.1.

Remember Dr. Robert Bullard from Chapter 1? Students can also learn more about Bullard through this video here: https://youtu.be/ynYHoPntckk?feature=shared. Together, Drs. Bullard and Wright developed an initiative utilizing the communiversity model, which has a specific emphasis on Historically Black Colleges and Universities (HBCUs). Most HBCUs are located in the South, particularly in the Gulf Coast and South Atlantic regions of the United States, which are characterized by extreme weather conditions, including droughts, heat waves, hurricanes, and flooding. Thus, Bullard and Wright developed the HBCU Climate Change Consortium. The consortium was founded in 2015 to raise awareness about the disproportionate impacts of climate change on marginalized communities…and has a mission to develop

Table 2.1 The Deep South Center for Environmental Justice

Location	New Orleans, Louisiana
Environmental Injustices Addressed	Through various internships and student programming, students have the opportunity to receive hands-on experience by immersing themselves in the work of frontline communities adversely impacted by environmental pollution and climate change.
Assisting Organization	The Deep South Center for Environmental Justice promotes the rights of all people to be free from environmental harm, particularly communities of color along the Mississippi River Chemical Corridor and the broader Gulf Coast Region.
Organization Resources	Deep South Center for Environmental Justice: https://dscej.org/ HBCU Climate Change Conference: https://dscej.org/project/hbcu-climate-change-conference/ Environmental Justice Storytellers Project: https://dscej.org/project/hbcu-climate-change-conference/ HBCU Environmental & Climate Justice Corps Summer Internship: https://dscej.org/project/hbcu-climate-change-conference/ HBCU Climate Change Consortium: https://dscej.org/project/hbcu-climate-change-conference/

HBCU students, leaders, scientists, and advocates on issues related to climate change. They care about the young leaders of today and tomorrow, like your students!

Among the numerous awards they have received during their long careers, the American Bar Association recently named the distinguished duo "Human Rights Heroes" for their education and advocacy work in the fight for environmental justice. Bullard and Wright are also excellent examples of collaboration and teamwork for students. Additionally, your students can create biographies of these leaders, as they are often not featured in school libraries. Students can create posters, use Book Creator, or make their own books. Or reach Bullard and Wright with their books! Another possibility is for students to start an environmental justice leaders section in the classroom or school library to catalog and showcase their learning.

The struggle for environmental justice and climate justice lies in the intersections of historic and present injustices and systems of oppression, like racism and settler colonialism, to name a few. Thus, the need to center frontline communities in decision-making and solutions is clear, and established leaders have dedicated their careers to finding solutions. Now that we have learned about Dr. Wright and have learned about her story and work, let us look at Step 2: Join the Mission.

Step 2: Join the Mission

> After young learners have background knowledge of the professionals and their mission/work, they will mimic the professionals' work by using age-appropriate tools. Students will collect data and use tools like professionals.

Here are three opportunities that are differentiated by grade level. However, they can be modified according to the needs and abilities of the class as well. Through these opportunities, students can engage with Dr. Wright's mission and subsequently join the mission. Standards alignment ideas are also provided:

1 **Fourth and Fifth Grade: Learn More about the 2023 Lawsuit by Cancer Alley Residents**
   What would you do if you were a resident of Cancer Alley? Furthermore, what role does the law play in seeking justice for public health emergencies? In the following activity, students can take on the role of community activists and environmental lawyers! In 2023, a landmark lawsuit filed in a Louisiana federal court by residents of "Cancer Alley" declared an "environmental public health emergency" (Juhasz, 2023). The lawsuit called for an end to new fossil fuel, heavy industry, and petrochemical plants, as well as related infrastructure, in St. James Parish. In resistance to these human rights violations and health violations, members of local environmental justice organizations and faith organizations filed the action against the local government, citing decades of environmental racism and the negligence of industrial facilities in predominantly Black communities like St. James. In Table 2.2, you will find a sample lesson idea suitable for third, fourth, or fifth graders.

2 **Third, Fourth, Fifth Grade: Explore "Sacrifice Zones" Maps Using ProPublica Data**
   Journalists and investigative reporters play a crucial role in the fight against environmental injustices, relaying vital information to

Table 2.2 Exploring the Environmental Racism Case

Resources to Explore	Questions about the Case for Students to Consider	Extension Ideas
For Students: • Press Conference: https://www.facebook.com/InclusiveLA/videos/229369202981850 • Court Case Timeline: https://ccrjustice.org/home/what-we-do/our-cases/inclusive-louisiana-mount-triumph-baptist-church-rise-st-james-v-st-0 **For Teachers:** • Press Release from the Center for Constitutional Rights: https://ccrjustice.org/home/press-center/press-releases/landmark-environmental-racism-case-cancer-alley-residents-argue • Southern Justice Rising: https://ccrjustice.org/home/what-we-do/issues/southern-justice-rising	• Why is this a civil rights case? (Also, see the video of Dr. Robert Bullard explaining the connections between civil rights and environmental justice.) • Who are the parties on both sides of the case? • What happened? • Which party initiated or started this case? • What is this party asking the court to decide? • What penalty, remedy, or solution are they seeking? • If this is an ongoing trial, what is the current status of the case? • What does the person need to prove to win? • What is the burden of proof?	• Is there an example of environmental racism or environmental injustice in your state, town, or city that is also a civil rights violation that should be tried in court? • Is there an example of environmental racism or environmental injustice in another state that is also a civil rights violation that should be tried in court? • Learn about environmental lawyers and civil rights lawyers and the important work that they do to promote environmental justice. • Students can write letters to the lawyers or residents in Louisiana as a writing extension activity.

the public. Students can take on the role of journalists and reporters in this activity! Explore Table 2.3 for ideas of how students can use this data, which includes interactive GIS maps of real environmental data from "sacrifice zones" around the country in "The Most Detailed Map of Cancer-Causing Industrial Air Pollution in the U.S." The map

Table 2.3 Explore "Sacrifice Zones" Maps Using ProPublica Data

Resources to Explore	Activities for Students	Extension Ideas
For Students and Teachers: • The Most Detailed Map of Cancer-Causing Industrial Air Pollution in the U.S." https://projects.propublica.org/toxmap/ • "Poison in the Air." https://www.propublica.org/article/toxmap-poison-in-the-air	"The Most Detailed Map of Cancer-Causing Industrial Air Pollution in the U.S." • The article mentions "hot spots" around the country. How many are there, and where are they? • Click on the maps and explore a "hot spot" near your state. It will take you to another page. Answer the following questions: a What is the population in this hotspot? b What are the top emitters of cancer-causing chemicals in this area? c Click on the button "See combined risk in a neighborhood nearby." What is the facility or "offender" in the nearby neighborhood?	Explore "hot spots" near your city: a Now, at the top of the page, there is a magnifying glass. Search for a city with a zip code that's in your town. What did you find? b How close is the nearest hotspot? Click the button that says "see hotspot." c What is the population in the hot spot? d What is the "offender" or "facility" that is causing this hot spot? Local Action: a Is your city government doing anything to address this hotspot? If not, should they? b Are there any local environmental groups or organizations that are assisting in this effort? c Does your city have a "Sustainability Plan?" Is this "hot spot" in the Sustainability Plan, and does the city have a multi-year plan to address it? If not, who can tell you that? Building Campaigns: a Are there any local journalists covering this issue? b Can you contact them to help you raise awareness about this issue?

also has a studio recording entitled "Poison in the Air," which students can listen to. Depending on the class's needs, the teacher can model the activities for the whole group, and the class can then work together on the activities. As another idea, if students have 1:1 devices or can work independently, the teacher can assign separate activities or extension ideas.

3   **Kindergarten, First, and Second Grade: Explore Environmental Justice Mapping Tools**

Younger students can also play the role of environmental justice detectives! These interactive GIS mapping tools provide a dataset that combines location with pollution levels, as well as health, demographic, and socioeconomic indicators. Because the datasets are color-coded, even kindergarteners can read this data. With the teacher's help, students can use the map to easily locate their current location, a specific address, or a nearby town, and then add various layers to investigate different questions related to health impacts. The teacher might project the data using the appropriate tool to the whole class using a projector and guide the students through the exploration. For example, read my article in *Rethinking Schools* entitled "Action Research for Environmental Justice in the Kindergarten Classroom" (Waite, 2022), which used Google Maps and CalEnviroScreen, a GIS tool that maps pollution. Below are environmental justice mapping tools and their corresponding state agency. If your state is not listed, the federal EPA tool is listed last in Table 2.4.

Now that students have had opportunities to learn about the environmental professional's work and mission and have engaged in age-appropriate activities to learn the skills and tools utilized by the environmental professional, Step 3 is up next: Extend the mission and take civic action! Time to take a look below.

Step 3: Extend the Mission and Take Civic Action

> Once young learners have built the skill set of the professional in Step 2, the students will synthesize that skill into their mission to take civic action. It can expand on the work that the professional is already doing, or the young learner can take on a new mission inspired by the work of the professional, and what the student is passionate about.

Table 2.4 State-Specific Environmental Justice Mapping Tools

State and Agency	Agency	Environmental Justice Mapping Tool	Learning Resources to Explore (If Available)
California	Office of Environmental Health Hazard Assessment (OEHHA)	CalEnviroScreen: https://oehha.ca.gov/calenviroscreen	Read my article in *Rethinking Schools*, "Action Research for Environmental Justice in the Kindergarten Classroom," to learn about how I have used CalEnviroScreen with kindergarteners. Article link: https://rethinkingschools.org/articles/action-research-for-environmental-justice-in-the-kindergarten-classroom/
Connecticut	Connecticut Institute for Resilience & Climate Adaptation (CIRCA)	Connecticut EJ Screening Tool: https://connecticut.maps.arcgis.com/apps/webappviewer/index.html?id=5adac07c27db40bbabc193af58634e5a	Fact Sheet and User Guide: https://connecticut-environmental-justice.circa.uconn.edu/fact-sheet/
Colorado	Colorado Department of Public Health and Environment (CDPHE)	Colorado EnviroScreen: https://cdphe.colorado.gov/enviroscreen	Colorado EnviroScreen Story Maps: https://cdphe.colorado.gov/colorado-enviroscreen-storymaps
North Carolina	North Carolina Department of Environmental Quality (DEQ)	Community Mapping System: https://ncdenr.maps.arcgis.com/apps/webappviewer/index.html?id=1eb0fbe2bcfb4cccb3cc212af8a0b8c8	Stakeholder Feedback Link: https://www.deq.nc.gov/outreach-education/environmental-justice/deq-north-carolina-community-mapping-system/deq-north-carolina-community-mapping-system-survey

(Continued)

Table 2.4 (Continued)

State and Agency	Agency	Environmental Justice Mapping Tool	Learning Resources to Explore (If Available)
New Jersey	New Jersey Department of Environmental Protection	New Jersey Environmental Justice Mapping, Assessment, and Protection Tool (EJMAP): https://experience.arcgis.com/experience/548632a2351b41b8a0443cfc3a9f4ef6	Students can scroll through the StoryMap in the Map itself, in the link to the left
Michigan	Michigan Department of Environment, Great Lakes, and Energy	MiEJScreen: https://egle.maps.arcgis.com/apps/webappviewer/index.html?id=b100011f137945138a52a35ec6d8676f	N/A
Federal	US EPA	EJScreen: https://www.epa.gov/ejscreen	User Guide: https://www.epa.gov/ejscreen/learn-use-ejscreen

In Step 3, one idea is to have students investigate environmental injustices in their local community or their state. Using the various GIS tools from Step 2, students now have real environmental data and "language" to support their arguments. They can design campaigns to spread awareness and encourage action, integrating digital learning, mixed media, art, and writing. Students can also interview environmental activists, elders, or environmental professionals in their community. There are endless possibilities! While frontline communities have been fighting for social justice, civil rights, and environmental justice for decades, a larger question remains: What is climate justice, and what are the public's perceptions and attitudes about climate justice? What does this mean for your professional practice as you begin to teach about environmental justice? A research group, the Yale Program on Climate Change Communication, has been investigating this question.

Climate Justice and Communicating to Stakeholders

However, wait, what is climate justice? Now that you know about environmental justice and have learned about the Environmental Justice Movement and some of its history, think of climate justice as a continuation of that and a connecting bridge. For example, climate justice connects the goals of the decades-long environmental justice and climate change movements to address how climate change disproportionately impacts people who are already more vulnerable to its impacts. This vulnerability can be due to personal factors at the individual level (such as age, income, or disability) and/or social factors at the larger systemic level (such as racism and other forms of oppression). Thus, climate justice addresses the disproportionate impacts of climate change by prioritizing the safety and health of those who face the most significant risk in frontline communities. Environmental justice and climate justice focus on developing community-driven solutions that address the root causes and systemic issues. Time to learn more!

Two leaders we learned about, like Drs. Robert Bullard and Beverly Wright, believe that environmental justice means "the community should be made whole" (Curwood, 2024). Thus, the solutions and approaches must come from the people in the communities who are directly impacted, and a restorative approach is necessary. This "community-centered approach" to environmental justice means embracing the residents' lived experiences, community knowledge, and community assets. Think about the community where your school is. What forms of community knowledge might your students have? What are some other reasons why it might be essential to involve residents of all ages in the solutions process? Now, think of outside organizations that come into the community and utilize "top-down" approaches, thrusting their agenda upon those who live there without their input. How would that make you feel, and why would that be problematic?

Many community organizers and leaders around the country are taking community-centered approaches to addressing environmental and climate injustices, including Black, Indigenous, and People of Color (BIPOC) and LGBTQIA+ activists, who we will learn about later in this chapter. Now that we have learned about climate justice, let us examine how the public perceives it. This is essential information for teachers because it is necessary to understand how the American public views specific issues and how that relates to your school context. As a result, this ultimately determines how you can teach about equity and social justice issues. It also determines how you communicate with parents and your school administrators. Let us dig in!

Public Perceptions of Climate Change

One of the most essential communication rules is knowing your audience. The Yale Program on Climate Change Communication (YPCCC) researches public knowledge of climate change, policy preferences, attitudes, behaviors, and the underlying psychological, political, and cultural factors that influence them. They also "engage the public in climate change science and solutions, in partnership with governments, media organizations, companies, and civil society, and with a daily, national radio program, Yale Climate Connections" (Yale Program on Climate Change Communication [YPCCC], n.d.). One of YPCCC's signature research contributions is the framework entitled *Global Warming's Six Americas* (Leiserowitz et al., 2013), based on the understanding that individuals have different political, cultural, and psychological reasons for how they think and act on climate change. "Six Americas" refers to six distinct audience archetypes that represent six unique ways the American public responds to climate change. They are as follows: Alarmed, concerned, cautious, disengaged, doubtful, and dismissive. After examining Table 2.5, which of the Six Americas do you fall under? How about other teachers at

Table 2.5 The Six Americas

Audience (Highest Belief to Lowest Belief)	Description of Audience
Alarmed	Convinced that global warming is happening and recognizing that it is a threat caused by humans, they support climate change policies.
Concerned	They believe human-caused global warming is happening, but they tend to think climate impacts are not occurring now, so it is not a high-priority issue for them.
Cautious	Unsure and undecided: Not sure if it is happening, serious, or human-caused.
Disengaged	Know little about the topic, and have not heard about it in the media.
Doubtful	Do not think global warming is happening at all. Do not give it much thought or consider it a serious risk.
Dismissive	Do not believe global warming is happening. Do not believe it is human-caused, or a threat—the most likely to endorse conspiracy theories.

your school or district? Take the short quiz here to find out: https://climate communication.yale.edu/visualizations-data/sassy/.

Over the past ten years, the group that has increased in size compared to other groups is alarmed, and it has nearly doubled! The group that has decreased in size is the cautious group. Moreover, the percentage of Americans who are either alarmed or concerned has increased from 40% in 2013 to 56% in 2023. Disengaged and dismissive have remained relatively stable over the past decade. What does this show us? This evidence suggests the American public is concerned about global warming! Growing more concerned over time raises the larger question: What do Americans want to know about climate change? If you could ask a scientist a question about climate change, what would you ask? Overall, 44% of Americans are most interested in learning about solutions to global warming (Ballew et al., 2024). However, what about solutions to the disproportionate impacts of climate change?

Public Perceptions of Climate Justice

As we learned, climate justice is a fundamental component of addressing climate change. The communities most affected by climate change and other environmental disasters are those least responsible for causing it. Across the Six Americas, there is recognition of climate injustices. Around half of Americans (49%) agree that climate change harms some groups in the United States more than others. Additionally, about one in three Americans (34%) agree that a history of racist policies makes people of color more likely than white people to be harmed by global climate change. Which Six Americas groups would be the most concerned about climate justice? How about the least concerned? Why might that be? Find out in Table 2.5.

The Alarmed, followed by the Concerned, are the most likely to think global warming harms some groups more than others, are more likely to support climate justice goals, and to vote for pro-justice candidates. In addition, a large majority of the Alarmed are more likely to recognize the disproportionate environmental harms based on socioeconomic status and race. On the other hand, the Doubtful and Dismissive are the least likely to acknowledge existing climate injustices or to support climate justice. The overall significance is that the audiences most worried about climate change (approximately 56% Alarmed or Concerned) are also the most likely to support goals aimed at advancing climate justice. Thus, there is substantial evidence in support of climate justice. Although there is high support, awareness is low. As a teacher, you recognize that parents and administrators are essential audiences for climate change and climate justice communication. You are probably wondering how I communicate with parents about climate change.

How about communicating with administrators or other school officials? No worries, I have you covered!

Communicating with Parents

Parents want to talk to their kids about climate change, but often lack the knowledge on how to do so and need support to approach the topic with their children. Thus, activities for teachers and students are very effective and can also be great ways to increase and strengthen community and school involvement. Here are some strategies for communicating with parents:

- Listen when parents bring you concerns or questions. Always acknowledge their concerns and validate feelings.
- Showcase examples of how climate change, environmental justice, or climate justice show up in your class, emphasizing age-appropriate content and activities that are standards-aligned.
- Emphasize that teaching about climate change, environmental justice, or climate justice empowers students with the tools to make informed choices and act, thus giving them self-determination.
- Connect parents to local climate action initiatives or community-based organizations.
- Showcase ways that students are learning to think critically, use real scientific data, and learn about solutions and innovations related to our changing planet.

While parents might seem like a piece of cake, let us tackle a bigger challenge: Talking to your school or district administration, whether you speak to your principal, a curriculum specialist, your vice principal, your superintendent, or in front of a school board meeting, here are some ideas below to help you advocate, feel empowered, prepared, and confident!

Communicating with School and District Administration and Leadership

- *There Is Power in Numbers*: There is power in numbers, and do not teach in a silo! Connect with other teachers at your school site or school district who share common interests, or connect with community groups that advocate for and conduct outreach on environmental and/or climate justice teaching. For example, the Zinn Education Project runs various campaigns and coalitions for social justice education, including Teach Climate Justice. The link is here: https://www.zinnedproject.org/campaigns/teach-climate-justice.

- ◆ *Know the Numbers*: Arming yourself with statistics and data is often very effective. For example, a study by Will and Prothero (2022) found that parental support for climate change education is around 80%. Additionally, an NPR/Ipsos poll reveals that a substantial majority of US teachers (86%) and parents (84%) support incorporating climate change education into school curricula (Kamenetz, 2019).
- ◆ *Know Your Audience*: Thinking About the YPCCC "Six Americas," research your school district's curriculum guidelines and any existing policies; Tailor your approach to address any existing concerns of parents, administrators, or community members before a meeting or discussion.
- ◆ *Offer Solutions*: Present ideas for integrating climate change, environmental justice, or climate justice into the curriculum. Emphasize how researchers have found that a critical consciousness can improve academic achievement (mentioned in Chapter 1). Also, emphasize that what you do helps increase student engagement with the content standards and critical thinking.
- ◆ *Do Not Give Up*: As teachers committed to social justice and equity, we know that teaching for justice is often an uphill battle. Be persistent! When you feel discouraged, don't give up; instead, reach out to your community. If you are working alone on this project at your school, Climate Generation is also a great group to connect with, offering summer institutes and webinars. Their link is here: https://climategen.org/

Now that we have a toolkit of strategies and tools for communicating with parents and school officials, let us continue to learn more about climate justice and where youth activists have been carving out their spaces.

Student Activism: The Education That Students Are Fighting For

While youth climate activists have captivated the world's attention, the student-led climate activist movement began forming in Australia as early as 1991 with the Students of Sustainability. Additional student-led efforts include the Student Environmental Network, the Australian Youth Climate Coalition (2006), and the Indigenous Youth Climate Network Seed Mob (2014). Since 2014, youth-led climate coalitions have been forming in other countries, like the UK Youth Climate Coalition, the Canadian Youth Climate Coalition, and the Indian Youth Climate Coalition. In the United States, the *Rethinking Schools* student movement launched its climate activist school-based organizing toolkit in 2016 in Portland, Oregon. Notably, in 2018, the world's attention turned to Greta Thunberg, the 15-year-old Swedish student activist who was protesting at her country's parliament for hours with a *Skolstrejk för klimatet* (School Strike for Climate) sign instead of going to school. Today's students are walking out of school, which has often failed to address and respond to their concerns, and go beyond just curriculum and instruction. Our climate emergency also has severe implications for school building infrastructure and the conditions of teaching and learning.

Extreme Heat and Learning Loss

Since 2022, approximately 400 million students worldwide have experienced school closures due to extreme heat, resulting in detrimental effects on students in low-income areas and underfunded schools. In 2024, the average ten-year-old will have experienced three times more floods, five times more droughts, and 36 times more heatwaves than a one-year-old in 1970 (Sabarwal et al., 2024). Additionally, today's students are more likely to experience school closures, and schools may need to quickly shift between in-person and remote learning modalities. School leaders and administrators cannot ignore these issues as they impact school and district budgets regarding infrastructure, power, and utilities. Has your school or district experienced extreme weather events? How did this affect your teaching and your students' learning?

Does your school district or city have a sustainability plan? Your student researchers can investigate! Columbia University's Center for Sustainable Future and the Public Matters Project (Pizmony-Levy et al., 2023) conducted a nationally representative survey of more than 2,000 adults. The study found that 85% of respondents somewhat or strongly agreed that schools should install solar panels and source food from local providers. Three-quarters said schools should use more energy-efficient electric equivalents instead of diesel buses. Three-quarters of respondents also said marginalized communities must be prioritized in schools' climate change efforts. However, researchers LeRoy et al. (2021) from the Center for Climate Integrity found that equipping all public schools in the United States with modern air conditioning systems that last an average of 20 years would cost approximately $42 million. Extreme heat is also problematic for schools due to the effects on concentration and slower cognitive function.

Have you had to teach in extreme temperatures? If so, how was it for you and your students? A study of school-age children in the United States, England, Sweden, and Denmark found the temperature for optimal concentration is 72 degrees Fahrenheit. School performance on tests and other learning tasks can increase by about 20% if classroom temperatures are lowered from 86 degrees Fahrenheit to 68 degrees Fahrenheit (Wargocki et al., 2019). In addition, Harvard University's Early Childhood Scientific Council on Equity and the Environment (2023) found that learning losses increased by up to 50% in New York City when school day temperatures went above 100 degrees Fahrenheit compared to days above 90 degrees Fahrenheit. Is your school or district equipped to handle extreme temperatures?

Also, extreme weather that disrupts schools can be particularly devastating for students with special needs. For example, due to school closures, students with disabilities who end up being displaced from schools or have to transfer mid-year may fall even further behind in their learning than their peers who do not have disabilities. This is especially problematic because emergency management agencies and school districts typically fail to integrate the needs of people with disabilities into the emergency management plans (National Council on Disability, 2023). Here are more resources to explore the impacts of climate change on people with disabilities:

- EPA Report: https://www.epa.gov/climateimpacts/climate-change-and-health-people-disabilities
- People with Disabilities Must Be Included in Climate Planning: https://hls.harvard.edu/today/people-with-disabilities-must-be-included-in-climate-planning-and-responses-say-harvard-researchers/

Elevating BIPOC and LGBTQIA+ Youth Activists

BIPOC communities are disproportionately impacted by climate change in the United States. Children from frontline communities are especially vulnerable to the health impacts of climate change. Youth from frontline communities are underrepresented within the environmental movement. To protect our planet, the input and contributions of as many people as possible must be incorporated, including BIPOC and LGBTQIA+ youth activists. More information about how the LGBTQIA+ community is disproportionately impacted by climate change will be discussed in Chapter 4. Learn about some amazing BIPOC and LGBTQIA+ activists to share with your students below.

Water Warriors

Learn about these youth activists in the United States and worldwide who use advocacy, art, and science to share how we can save our planet's rivers, oceans, and lakes. According to the United States Geological Survey, about 71% of the Earth's surface is water-covered. Thus, water conservation and access to water are becoming center-stage battles created by climate change. After looking at Table 2.6 for profiles of young water warriors you can bring

Table 2.6 Water Warriors to Share with Your Students

Name	About	Affiliation/Group
Victoria Barrett	In 2012, Victoria's school was flooded by Hurricane Sandy. She and 20 other plaintiffs decided to sue the government. Our Children's Trust filed. The lawsuit alleges that the U.S. government is violating children's Fifth Amendment right to life, liberty, and property by allowing fossil fuel burning to go unregulated; and that this inaction is discrimination against young people by valuing today's adults over young people who did not contribute to the climate crisis; and that this is negligence of the public trust doctrine.	Alliance for Climate Education: https://acespace.org/ Our Children's Trust: https://www.ourchildrenstrust.org/
Melati and Isabel Wijsen	Indonesian sisters founded the NGO Bye Plastic Bags, which is now active in nine countries. They had the idea due to their lived experiences growing up on an island and the lasting impact of single-use plastics. Two years after their initiative was founded, they received confirmation from the governor that Bali would be plastic-free by 2018.	Bye-Bye Plastic Bags: https://byebyeplasticbags.org/#home

(Continued)

Table 2.6 (*Continued*)

Name	About	Affiliation/Group
Jasilyn Charger	A water protector from the Cheyenne River Reservation, and founder of the International Indigenous Youth Council at Standing Rock. The camp of water protectors at Standing Rock was initiated by teenagers like Jasilyn, who helped launch the historic movement.	International Indigenous Youth Council: https://www.facebook.com/IIYCFamily/ The Youth Group That Launched a Movement at Standing Rock: https://www.nytimes.com/2017/01/31/magazine/the-youth-group-that-launched-a-movement-at-standing-rock.html?_r=0 Democracy Now Interview: https://www.democracynow.org/2017/1/4/from_keystone_xl_pipeline_to_dapl
Autumn Peltier	An Indigenous rights activist and designated "water protector," Autumn Peltier is the Chief Water Commissioner for the Anishinaabe Nation, and she has spent nearly half her life speaking about the importance of clean water to organizations, including the United Nations and the World Economic Forum.	CNN Feature: https://www.cnn.com/2022/08/09/americas/autumn-peltier-water-protector-first-nations-canada-spc/index.html
Kathy Jetñil-Kijiner	A poet, activist, and performance artist from the Marshall Islands. She co-founded the non-profit Jo-Jikum, which is dedicated to empowering Marshallese youth with tools to seek solutions to climate change and other environmental impacts.	Poetry Foundation: https://www.poetryfoundation.org/poets/kathy-jetnil-kijiner Jo-Jikum: https://www.localfutures.org/programs/global-to-local/planet-local/place-based-education/jo-jikum/

to your classroom community, check out the list below for ideas about integrating powerful change agents into your curriculum.

Here are some ideas for bringing these activists into your classroom:

- Teach the role of youth activism and youth activists at Standing Rock.
- Create biographies of the youth activists to share with students at your school or to add to your classroom library or school library.
- Create a book of Water Warriors to add to your classroom or school library.
- Investigate what other countries around the world have youth who are suing their government for accountability.
- How do single-use plastics and plastic pollution disproportionately affect low-income communities? Why is plastic pollution an environmental justice issue?
- Do other Indigenous Nations have Chief Water Commissioners? What does this role entail?
- Writing environmental justice and climate justice poetry and/or performing spoken word pieces.

Climate Creators

In the TikTok, Instagram, and Snapchat era, many young activists harness the power of digital literacy, education, and social media in their advocacy, outreach, and activism efforts. Some examples of climate creators are in Table 2.7. There are also ideas to bring these water warriors into your classroom community after the table.

How can your students harness the power of digital media, creativity, and communication to advance environmental justice and climate justice? Here are some ideas to harness their 21st-century skills and 21st-century learning:

Table 2.7 Climate Creators to Share with Your Students

Name	About	Social Media Handle
Helen Gualinga	An Indigenous land and human rights defender in the Ecuadorian Amazon. A member of the Indigenous Youth Collective of Amazon Defenders.	@Helenagualinga: https://www.instagram.com/helenagualinga/

(Continued)

Table 2.7 (Continued)

Name	About	Social Media Handle
Veronica Mulenga	A climate and environmental justice activist from Zambia who uses her platform to raise awareness about the climate crisis, environmental injustice, and the disproportionate impacts of climate change. Additionally, Veronica is part of the @YouthClimateSave movement, a global youth-led organization that addresses the connection between agriculture and the climate crisis. She also organizes the @YouthClimateSaveZambia chapter.	@veronicamulenga: https://www.instagram.com/veronicamulenga_/?hl=en
Maya Penn	A Gen Z environmental justice activist, TED Talk speaker, and artist. Among her notable achievements was creating the first-ever digital report presented to the US Congress. Maya received a commendation from President Obama for Outstanding Achievement in Environmental Stewardship.	@Mayasideas: https://www.instagram.com/mayasideas/

- Use Google Slides or Google Drawings to make biographies or profiles of youth environmental justice and climate justice activists.
- Use Book Creator to create a book about environmental injustices in their local community.
- Use Canva to create infographics for an awareness campaign for the school, city, or community.

Now What? How This Book Can Help

Congratulations! You have finished Part 1: Getting Started—What Do I Need to Know to Teach About Environmental Justice? You have learned about the Principles of Environmental Justice for K-5 Students and their corresponding elements. After learning from Kindergarten Environmental Justice Researchers and Second-Grade Water Justice Investigators, I hope you see how teaching about environmental justice and climate justice can and should be incorporated into elementary school curricula. Elementary school students are not only highly capable of learning about these issues, but their strong sense of right and wrong makes them highly invested and engaged in the topics. Also, as elementary school teachers and educators committed to equity and social justice, you are primed to teach about environmental justice and climate justice because they are not just "science" topics. Elementary teachers teach multiple subjects and possess a unique skill set to help students connect across disciplines, subjects, and content standards. As we progress through the book, there will be even more ways to think critically and act on disrupting the "green status quo" and "green business as usual." To reflect on what you learned in this first section, consider the following reflection questions about your professional practice. Before moving on, do not forget to check out the further reading section for resources for students and teachers from this chapter!

Reflection Questions for Professional Practice

Chapter 2 Questions

- Which of the Six Americas does your state, region, or school community fall under? How might this impact your ability to teach about climate change, climate justice, or environmental justice?
- How can students use digital literacy to communicate environmental and climate justice?
- What resources do you already have in your classroom that you can use to teach about water protectors? How can the youth activist profiles help?

Further Reading: Resources for Teachers and Students

Books for Teachers

Detraz, N. (2023). *Women and climate change: Examining discourses from the global North*. Cambridge, MA: MIT Press.

Flowers, C. C. (2020). *Waste: One woman's fight against America's dirty secret*. New York, NY: The New Press.

Hernandez, J. (2022). *Fresh banana leaves: Healing Indigenous landscapes through Indigenous science*. Berkeley, CA: North Atlantic Books.

Johnson, A. E., & Wilkinson, K. K. (Eds.). (2021). *All we can save: Truth, courage, and solutions for the climate crisis.* London: One World.

Kim, N. Y. (2021). *Refusing death: Immigrant women and the fight for environmental justice in LA.* Redwood City, CA: Stanford University Press.

Kimmerer, R. W. (2013). *Braiding sweetgrass: Indigenous wisdom, scientific knowledge, and the teachings of plants.* Minneapolis, MN: Milkweed Press.

McDuff, M. (2023). *Love your mother: 50 States, 50 stories, and 50 women united for climate justice.* Minneapolis, MN: Broadleaf Books.

Picture Books for Students

Bharara, P. (2022). *Justice is: A guide for young truth seekers.* New York, NY: Crown Books for Young Readers.

Chisholm, P. (2014). *Buried sunlight: How fossil fuels have changed the Earth.* Frederick, MD: The Blue Sky Press.

Douglass, P. (2022). *A kid's guide to saving the planet: It is not hopeless, and we are not helpless.* Minneapolis, MN: Beaming Books.

Fairbanks, A. (2024). *This land (race to the truth).* New York, NY: Crown Books for Young Readers.

Greenlaw, S., & Frey, G. (2021). *The first blade of sweetgrass.* Ann Arbor, MI: Tilbury House Publishers.

Stevens, G. (2021). *Climate action: The future is in our hands.* Wilton, CT: 360 Degrees.

References

Ballew, M., Verner, M., Carman, J., Myers, T., Rosenthal, S., Kotcher, J., Maibach, E., & Leiserowitz, A. (2024). *What do Americans want to know about climate change?* Yale University and George Mason University. New Haven, CT: Yale Program on Climate Change Communication.

Bullard, R. D. (2011). Sacrifice zones: The front lines of toxic chemical exposure in the United States. *Environmental Health Perspectives, 119*(6), A266. https://pmc.ncbi.nlm.nih.gov/articles/PMC3114843/

Curwood, S. (2024, February 24). *Q & A: Robert Bullard says 2024 is the year of environmental justice for an inundated Shiloh, Alabama.* Inside Climate News. https://insideclimatenews.org/news/24022024/robert-bullard-says-2024-is-year-of-environmental-justice-for-shiloh-alabama/#:~:text=%E2%80%9CIf%20we%20plan%20for%20environmental,we%20place%20everybody%20at%20risk.%E2%80%9D

Deen, A. (2021, November 30). *What happens when communities and universities teach each other? Communiversity.* Grist. https://grist.org/fix/justice/beverly-wright-communiversity-model-equitable-collaboration/

Early Childhood Scientific Council on Equity and the Environment. (2023). *Extreme heat affects early childhood development and health: Working Paper No. 1.* www.developingchild.harvard.edu

Human Rights Watch. (2024). *"We are dying here:' The fight for life in a Louisiana fossil fuel sacrifice zone.* https://www.hrw.org/report/2024/01/25/were-dying-here/fight-life-louisiana-fossil-fuel-sacrifice-zone

Juhasz, A. (2023, March 23). *Black residents of Louisiana file landmark lawsuit.* Human Rights Watch. https://www.hrw.org/news/2023/03/23/black-residents-louisiana-file-landmark-lawsuit

Kamenetz, A. (2019). Most teachers do not teach climate change; 4 in 5 parents wish they did. NPR. https://www.npr.org/2019/04/22/714262267/most-teachers-dont-teach-climate-change-4-in-5-parents-wish-they-did

Leiserowitz, A., Maibach, E., Roser-Renouf, C., Feinberg, G., & Howe, P. (2013). *Global warming's six Americas, September 2012.* New Haven, CT: Yale University and George Mason University. Yale Project on Climate Change Communication.

LeRoy, S., Matthews, M., & Wiles, R. (2021). *Hotter days, higher costs: The cooling crisis in America's classrooms.* The Center for Climate Integrity Resilience Analytics. https://coolingcrisis.org/uploads/media/HotterDaysHigherCosts-CCI-September2021.pdf

National Council on Disabilities. (2023, May 4). *The impacts of extreme weather events on people with disabilities.* National Integrated Heat Health Information System (NIHHIS).

Pizmony-Levy, O., Koch, P. A., & Rivet, A. E. (2023). *Green light for comprehensive climate change education.* Columbia University. https://doi.org/10.7916/jmzp-ay10

Sabarwal, S., Venegas Marin, S., Spivack, M. H., & Ambasz, D. (2024). Choosing our future-education for climate action. https://coilink.org/20.500.12592/4xm8v03

Wargocki, P., Porras-Salazar, J. A., & Contreras-Espinoza, S. (2019). The relationship between classroom temperature and children's performance in school. *Building and Environment, 157,* 197–204.

Waite, K. (2022). Action research for environmental justice in the kindergarten classroom. *Rethinking Schools, 36*(3).

Will, M., & Prothero, A. (2022, November 29). Teens know climate change is real. They want schools to teach more about it. *Education Week.* https://www.edweek.org/teaching-learning/teens-know-climate-change-is-real-they-want-schools-to-teach-more-about-it/2022/11#:~:text=Sixty%2Dfive%20percent%20of%20the,understand%20the%20science%20behind%20it.

Yale Program on Climate Change Communication (YPCCC). (n.d.). *What we do.* https://climatecommunication.yale.edu/

Part 2

The First Steps—Shifting the Focus from Mainstream Environmentalism to Environmental Justice

Part 2 provides a foundation for understanding why we must shift from mainstream environmentalism to teaching and learning about environmental injustices. In Chapter 3, learn why it is essential to shift the focus from mainstream environmentalism to environmental justice and develop strategies and tools to challenge the "green status quo" and "green business as usual." We will continue exploring Principle 1: Encourage Student Questions and Observations, with an emphasis on Element 2: Aim to Cultivate and Develop a Critical Consciousness. Learn from fifth-grade National Park truth detectives who uncover the true history behind our National Park system. Additionally, learn about environmental professionals like J. Drew Lanham, who utilize multiple disciplines in their work, which aligns with the Learning for Justice Social Justice Standards.

In this chapter, we delve into the concept of intersectionality, which highlights the need to address environmental justice in conjunction with factors such as race, class, socioeconomic status, gender, sexual orientation, and other social identities. We will learn how different populations disproportionately experience environmental injustices, dive into a new kind of Gen-Z activism, and explore how musicians use their platforms for environmental activism. We will continue learning about Principle 2: Not Just a Science Issue, and Principle 3: In Community with Elders, Activists, and Environmental Professionals. This chapter's spotlight focuses on fourth-grade natural disaster analysts who want to use songs to save the planet! At the end of both chapters, check out the additional resources for teachers and students.

DOI: 10.4324/9781003620709-5

3

Shifting from Mainstream Environmentalism to Environmental Justice

Spotlight: Fifth-Grade National Park Truth Detectives

It was the week before spring break. Mr. Lee's fifth graders suddenly returned to class after lunch. The excitement hung in the thick, humid air as students discussed their vacation plans and loudly chatted with their table groups.

Donna, one of the table captains, said to the class, "Hey, you all, look! Look! SHHHHHHHHHH!!! Hey, you all! SHHHHHHHH!" She threw the silent signal with her fingers and looked at Mr. Lee. The rest of her table did the same. The classroom became quiet as the rest of the students also raised their quiet signal with their fingers.

"Thank you, Donna, and table 5," said Mr. Lee. "I will give you some table points." He walked towards the whiteboard and added points to their points jar. As he turned around, Mr. Lee could feel the students' excessive energy as the days drew near to vacation. He let out another sigh. He knew he had to find a way to channel that energy into a positive outlet. He had an idea!

"Okay, class, you are all excited for spring break. So we will talk about that! I remember many of you planned to visit some National Parks during the vacation." He saw many heads nod in agreement.

"Discuss with your table groups which National Parks you know of or which National Parks you plan to visit during spring break. What will you do, or what would you want to do? I will give you three minutes to discuss, and please keep this at level 3 on the noise meter," said Mr. Lee as he pointed to the noise meter on the whiteboard.

DOI: 10.4324/9781003620709-6

"Okay, class, so I heard some great conversations about the National Parks you will visit or the Parks you are interested in visiting. Can two table captains share an example of what your group talked about?"

Tammy raised her hand, and Mr. Lee nodded at her. "Mr. Lee, we talked about Everglades National Park and Biscayne National Park. We want to see alligators!" Her table group nodded eagerly in agreement.

"Excellent work, everyone," said Mr. Lee.

Now that we have brainstormed and have some initial ideas, that brings us to our social studies lesson for today. Today we are going to be truth detectives, and we are going to learn more about the history of the National Parks.

"To be truth detectives all year and across all of our subjects, we have also been learning about the three components of critical consciousness." Mr. Lee pointed to a poster on the wall that had a pie chart depicting the three components of critical consciousness: (1) Social analysis, (2) Political agency, and (3) Social action.

"Today we are going to work on our social analysis," he said. Several heads bobbed up and down.

We will watch this clip from the PBS documentary, The National Parks: America's Best Idea. When watching, please fill out this graphic organizer to help you process the information. After we watch the clip, you will have time to discuss it in your table groups.

Okay, class, when you are watching, make sure to be truth detectives and look for these critical questions that we have on the graphic organizer. Remember, these questions are helping us to develop and refine our social analysis, and they are on the wall over there. Time to review them: 1) Whose perspective is reflected in the idea of the National Parks; 2) Whose perspective is absent; 3) Whose interests are served by the founding of the National Parks; 4) Whose are not; 5) How are different people portrayed or constructed in this narrative/idea; 6) What could be problematic about this narrative/idea?

The fifth graders eagerly wrote on their graphic organizers as the documentary clip played. After the clip was finished, Mr. Lee said,

Okay, now I am going to give you ten minutes at your table group to compare answers and finish your graphic organizer, and then we will discuss it as a class. Please remember to keep the volume at level 3 on the noise meter.

After the time was up, Mr. Lee brought the class back to attention. "Okay, let us start with table 2. What did the detectives find out?"

"Well, Mr. Lee...we definitely got some answers!" said Shirley, who sat up straight and put her shoulders back as she looked at her tablemates. "Didn't we learn last week about the Indigenous peoples? About the different tribes and their governments...well, we did not see any Indigenous peoples in this clip...like, aren't there Indigenous peoples everywhere?" Her table groups eagerly nodded in agreement.

"Okay, table 3. What did you find?" Rebecca sat up straight.

Mr. Lee...that one guy, John Muir, well...sounds like he did some good things and was famous and loved nature and the mountains and whatnot, but like...he just made parks with the help of the President, but like were not the Indigenous peoples living there before that guy came there? Maybe they were already using it. Seems rude.

"Table 4, go ahead," said Mr. Lee, nodding at the table captain. "Yeah, Mr. Lee," said Harmony,

We learned in science last week about how the Indigenous peoples use plants as medicine and have their governments and other stuff like that and they care for the land and they know all about the land since they been there for infinity...but don't that mean they can take care of the land themselves since they been doing it for like, infinity? This guy just came in and wanted to take care of it for them, making a bunch of new rules for the land and other things. Yeah, that is rude! That is not right!

"YEAH!" said a chorus of voices across the room.

"Marvelous work, my detectives!" said Mr. Lee enthusiastically. "That brings us to our lesson for today. We are going to talk about opinion/argument writing today. I will pass out some materials for your tables that you can all look at."

"Here is a timeline of national parks. I have printed this out for you from the PBS website. I have also enlarged, printed out, and laminated some historical pictures from the documentary for you to look at. Table captains, please come and get these for your table. Talk about opinion/argument writing. Remember, here is the rubric we are using. Remember, a rubric tells you what you must do to succeed. The rubric is 0–4, 0 being the lowest and 4 being the highest. Time to review the rubric." Heads nodded in agreement.

Now that we have seen the fifth-grade National Park truth detectives in action, it is time to unpack some key takeaways from the lesson: The entry point was the teacher capitalizing on students' excessive energy before school vacation. All the teachers have been there! As a way to harness and focus his students' energy and enthusiasm about discussing spring break plans, Mr. Lee used that as a catalyst for his lesson on the history of the National Parks system. The lesson covered social studies, speaking and listening, and writing. Like Mr. Gomez in Chapter 2, Mr. Lee also employed the best practice of "table groups" or "think-pair-share," which provides a safe space for students to explore and discuss ideas with their peers before bringing them to a whole-group discussion. This provides scaffolding and support for students who are introverted and for English Language Learners. Additionally, through this practice, Mr. Lee was addressing Principle 1: Encourage Student Questions and Observations, Element 1: Facilitate Crucial Conversations All Year, and Element 2: Aim to Cultivate and Develop a Critical Consciousness.

To address Elements 1 and 2, Mr. Lee had a great poster on his classroom wall that illustrated the three components of critical consciousness. He related it to his lesson reviewing components with students. This is something you can create for your classroom wall, which will provide students with the necessary vocabulary. Mr. Lee also shared with students a series of "critical questions" he had on his classroom wall as a poster. These "critical questions" help students center criticality in the classroom throughout the year by analyzing which perspectives are centered and which are missing. These questions also provide a language that students can use to further develop and refine their social analysis and critique the status quo, especially the "green status quo." In addition to a classroom poster, another idea is to have these questions written on sentence strips for younger students or on note cards to keep at table groups if they have a shared pencil box of supplies. From the vignette, it is clear that the fifth graders had already practiced with these questions, as they could use them as an analytical framework easily, which means Mr. Lee regularly incorporates them into class routines and culture.

As a next step, Mr. Lee showed students some primary source documents about the history of the National Parks system, which addressed Principle 2: Not Just a Science Issue, and Element 1: Engagement and Entry Points Across the Curriculum. These resources are listed at the end of this chapter under the "Further Reading" section. You can print them out like Mr. Lee did, or if students have devices at their tables, they can explore the resources digitally. Another option would be for students to visit the computer lab for part of this assignment or work in groups to further research the primary source documents provided. To expand upon the opinion/argument goal of the writing assignment, students could also role-play or debate this topic. Note that Mr. Lee has given students the tools to analyze this history. The students have been given primary source documents to help support their arguments, and they have formed their own opinions based on the evidence, discussing them with their peers. This activity is aligned with content standards in Common Core speaking and listening, social studies, and/or history, and writing. All of this "evidence" can be used to justify a lesson on teaching the truth if needed.

To expand upon this lesson, teachers can also choose to show the video from *Grist*, an environmental news outlet, which is also listed in the "Further Reading" section, entitled *How Can We Make National Parks Accessible to Everybody*. This video shares historical examples and real data about the racial demographics of park visitors. Students will recognize John Muir's video quote. The narrator also addresses the histories of Indigenous removal and dispossession, and racial segregation within the National Parks. As an extension, the teacher could discuss the "landback" movement, which is a movement that calls for reparations for centuries of land theft and the return of land to Indigenous stewardship. This is important because the establishment of the National Parks system led to not only a loss of Indigenous homelands but also solidified ideas in the American consciousness about what constitutes the "environment" and "wilderness." We will discuss this later in this chapter and how the environmental justice movement sought to re-shift the focus to prioritize people over wilderness preservation and conservation. Now, time to continue with the great work that Mr. Lee and the fifth graders were doing. We should examine Principles 1 and 2 closely: Encourage Student Questions and Observations and Aim to Cultivate and Develop a Critical Consciousness. We will begin with Earth Day.

Rethinking Earth Day and Earth Month

Historical Foundation

When I was in elementary school, I had mixed feelings about April. In most elementary schools around the country, April is the "green month," or "Earth month." From my eight- and nine-year-old perspective, it never made sense that we would only celebrate the Earth once a year. Wasn't 12 months a year? If the Earth is so important, shouldn't we be doing things all year round? The Earth should have a birthday party all year! This made more sense to me because I celebrated all year! In elementary school, my most prized possessions were recycled jam jars where I stored my "treasures." I used to collect sea glass, rocks, shells, and twigs from the beaches and parks. Once they were full, I carefully arranged the jars along my bedroom windowsill. In the morning and early evenings, I would always watch with awe, fascination, wonder, and pure joy as the light from the sun hit the glass jars, danced across the wall in a rainbow explosion, and my wonderful treasures became illuminated like jewels. This sense of awe, wonder, and delight is one of the reasons I love the environment and one of the many reasons I enjoy teaching elementary students. When I told this story to my kindergarteners, many of them began bringing rocks, twigs, and other treasures to school in their lunchboxes throughout the year. However, when I learned about the modern U.S. environmental movement in school, I felt very separated and distant from it, and I felt no connection with the green founders. The four people positioned as the "founders" of the modern U.S. environmental movement, typically taught about or mentioned in classrooms around the country, are Rachel Carson, Senator Gaylord Nelson, Denis Hayes, and John Muir. First, learn about Rachel Carson, Senator Gaylord Nelson, and Denis Hayes.

Several factors contributed to the emergence of the modern U.S. environmental movement. In 1962, Rachel Carson's book *Silent Spring* was published, shifting public consciousness. It became a New York Times bestseller, boldly exposing the hazards of pesticides and the links between pollution and public health. It was scandalous at the time because Carson criticized the U.S. government for not considering the negative consequences of large-scale efforts that spread pesticides from farms to neighborhoods in the United States. Carson also wanted to lift the curtain and expose the issue so lawmakers and policymakers would restrict the use of pesticides. Moreover, Senator Gaylor Nelson from Wisconsin was also concerned about environmental issues in the United States. He said it was time to "get the nation to wake up and pay attention to the most important challenge the human species faces on the planet" (United States Senate, n.d., para. 3). Then, in 1969, he and the rest of America saw the detrimental impacts of an oil spill in Santa Barbara, which was caused by a well blowout. After visiting the area, he was inspired by the citizens who rallied together to initiate cleanups and the momentum of the student anti-war protests. He thought this same model of activism could be applied to leverage the American public's concern with water and air pollution. As a next step, he needed a group of dedicated young people to help spread the message about his cause.

After returning to Washington and discussing these ideas with his staff, Senator Nelson envisioned a grassroots movement and established an office staffed by college students and law students. Law student Denis Hayes was in charge of this youth group. Have you ever wondered why April is "Earth Month" or why Earth Day is in April? The young people identified April as an ideal time for a teach-in due to the favorable weather during this month, and also because it was a good time for college students, as it fell between spring break and college exams. Hayes established a national staff of 85 people to promote these events nationwide. Thus, April 22, 1970, became the first

Earth Day, and people around the country took to parks, the streets, classrooms, and auditoriums to celebrate and protest the impacts of 150 years of industrial development and the corresponding negative impacts on human health. Earth Day was celebrated by about "20 million Americans on 2,000 [college] campuses, at 10,000 primary and secondary schools, and in hundreds of communities" (United States Senate, n.d., para. 4). Subsequently, at the end of 1970, this first Earth Day led to the creation of the U.S. Environmental Protection Agency and the establishment of other environmental laws, like the National Environmental Education Act, the Occupational Safety and Health Act, and the Clean Air Act. Two years later, Congress passed the Clean Water Act. Thus, Earth Day is widely regarded as the birth of the modern U.S. environmental movement. However, while the date for Earth Day was student-driven, as a student myself, I still felt disconnected from this "green history."

As an eight-year-old elementary school student, I could understand on a logical level why we celebrate Earth Day, why environmental conservation is important, why we need laws and policies to protect the Earth from harmful substances like chemicals, and, of course, why species preservation is crucial. I also always wondered why everyone became obsessed with Bald Eagles and Polar Bears in April. These are great animals, but they seemed so far removed from my everyday experience. I did not think I would ever see a polar bear wandering around in my neighborhood! That would be really cool, though! I also wondered, what does a polar bear have to do with me and my lived experience? Also, when we learned about these great "environmentalists" in school, the founders of Earth Day and the environmental movement, well...they looked nothing like me. They were all white. When our teacher read picture books in class about Earth Day or environmentalism, the characters were also usually white. As an Asian American, I was used to not seeing myself reflected in the school curriculum in general. However, this invisibility and erasure were only further magnified because I experienced a disconnect between my love of the environment and school.

I received the message in school that an environmentalist is a white person, and therefore, by default, I am not an environmentalist. This eventually deterred my love of science and the environment and diminished my confidence in learning about this topic as I began to see myself separate and distant from it. As I grew older, what I loved most about the natural world was diminished by lessons that involved memorizing facts in long and boring textbooks. It was not until I became a public school teacher that my passion for the environment was re-energized. In particular, it was when I saw the joy and wonder that I experienced as a child reflected on my kindergarten students' faces when we were doing hands-on environmental projects.

However, I realized there was yet another educational disconnect, and this time, my predominantly Black and Brown students were also experiencing it. Learn more about that and how the Learning for Justice Social Justice Standards can help you teach for/about environmental justice.

Centering Students' Lived Experiences: Using the Learning for Justice Standards

Learning for Justice Social Justice Standards Overview

Learning for Justice (formerly Teaching Tolerance) is an initiative of the Southern Poverty Law Center. The Learning for Justice Social Justice Standards are written for K-12 audiences and have four domains: Identity, Diversity, Justice, and Action (Learning for Justice, 2022). Using these domains is a powerful way to center students' lived experiences, personal stories, and family histories. These domains have been specifically adapted and modified to relate to environmental justice and how we teach about the environment. Specifically, we will focus on Domains 1, 3, and 4: Identity, Justice, and Action.

Domain 1: Identity

In Domain 1: Identity, teachers provide students with opportunities to learn about their origins and their identities. The intention behind this is to reduce bias as students learn about their privileges, responsibilities, and identities. The overarching goal is to develop positive social identities and understand how these multiple identities overlap and intersect to create multidimensional individuals. A student's sense of self is important in learning about environmental justice and diverse narratives about our planet. As I unfortunately experienced in my schooling, not all students' environmental knowledge is seen as valuable in our dominant education system, as the environmental movement has been predominantly white. Table 3.1 outlines the actions teachers can take to help deepen students' understanding of their identity, particularly in the context of teaching environmental justice.

Domain 3: Justice

The justice domain focuses on the root causes and the structural causes of inequities. As teachers committed to equity and social justice, we can reflect on how these inequities and systems of oppression in the larger society are then replicated and reproduced to perpetuate the disproportionate impacts of environmental harms based on gender, race, socioeconomic status, ability,

Table 3.1 Identity Domain in Teaching Environmental Justice

Teachers Will:
- View students as competent and ensure that their lived experiences and community and cultural ways of knowledge/knowing are elevated, acknowledged, and leveraged in the teaching of environmental justice.
- Deconstruct negative stereotypes about children's environmental identities and negative stereotypes about who can and who cannot learn about environmental justice.
- Elevate and recenter the knowledge, identities, traditions, and perspectives about the environment that have been historically silenced.
- Honor and acknowledge students' multiple and intersectional identities in the design and implementation of the curriculum.

Students Will:
- Recognize that people's intersectional identities interact and create unique and complex ways that people contribute to the Environmental Movement, environmental justice, and climate justice activism.
- Express pride, confidence, and self-esteem about themselves and their community as environmental justice thinkers and learners.
- Develop historical and cultural knowledge to affirm and describe membership in multiple identity groups and their contributions to the Environmental Justice Movement.
- Recognize the traits of the dominant culture, their own culture, and other cultures, and how to negotiate their identity in multiple spaces.

etc. More will be covered in Chapter 5. As teachers, we also need to provide students with multiple pathways and entry points to recognize that privilege and power impact how people experience and relate to the environment, and how oppression in the environmental space can operate at both systemic and individual levels. Table 3.2 outlines actions that teachers can take to help deepen students' understanding of these systems of oppression and utilize justice as a response, specifically in the context of teaching about environmental justice.

Domain 4: Action in Environmental Justice Education

In Domain 4: Action in Environmental Justice Education, students have the opportunity to reflect on social movements for environmental justice (and other related movements, given the history of environmental justice) and work to take action to address these issues. Students can also identify topics of environmental justice that they are passionate about in their local communities, and at the state, regional, or national level. Students can practice

Table 3.2 Justice Domain in Teaching Environmental Justice

Teachers Will:
- Locate and recognize the root causes of injustices in social conditions, rather than believing conditions are inherent within individuals.
- Recognize that injustices are perpetuated in how environmental impacts like climate change are experienced based on race, class, gender, etc.
- Position frontline communities' perspectives, identities, and knowledge traditions as valuable.

Students Will:
- Recognize that stereotypes based on race, gender, class, etc., impact who is considered good at science and capable of working towards environmental justice solutions.
- Environmental justice education and climate justice education can be tools for identifying the inequitable impacts of climate change at the systemic level.

Table 3.3 Action Domain in Teaching Environmental Justice

Teachers Will:
- Provide students with opportunities to recognize their responsibility to stand up to environmental and climate injustices.
- Understand that learning can occur from a problem-posing pedagogy, designed around doubt, fear, hopes, and questions naturally occurring when students think about and grapple with environmental justice.
- Engage in community—and place-based pedagogies and experiences that bridge social movements and community movements for environmental and climate justice.

Students Will:
- Plan and lead collective action that utilizes environmental justice to address broader issues of injustice.
- Make data-informed decisions about how and when to take a stand and make a difference in their community.
- Understand how systems of oppression function in environmental justice and feel empowered with tools to take meaningful steps towards action and change.

research skills with real environmental justice data, critically analyze, and question who has the power to change the "green status quo" and "green business as usual." Check Table 3.3 for more ideas.

Now that we have learned about the Learning for Justice Social Justice Standards, specifically how to apply Domains 1, 3, and 4, let us put some of this into practice. We will continue to address Principle 1: Encourage Student Questions and Observations, specifically Element 1: Facilitate Crucial Conversations All Year, and Element 2: Aim to Cultivate and Develop a Critical Consciousness. To do this, we will continue what the fifth-grade National Park truth detectives started, and we will critique John Muir and John Muir Day. As educators committed to social justice and equity, we will challenge the "green status quo" and push back against this "green business as usual."

Public Memory and John Muir

Whose Environmentalism

John Muir, the beloved conservationist, naturalist, and founder of the Sierra Club, is regarded as the "father of the National Parks." Today, his quotes still regularly appear on water bottles, posters, t-shirts, and various REI products, as this "rugged American hero" archetype continues to represent all things green, outdoors, and wilderness. America, especially California, loves John Muir! In 1976, the California Historical Society proclaimed John Muir to be "The Greatest Californian." In 1988, the U.S. government followed suit, and a U.S. Congressional Joint resolution designated April 21 to be "John Muir Day," since it marked John Muir's 150th birthday. Next, the 2004 California state quarter issued by the United States Mint depicted John Muir's image, and in 2017, California's Governor Brown issued a proclamation and declared April 21 as "John Muir Day" in the state of California. This is even reflected in California's Education Code Section 37222, which is about days in the school calendar that have special significance (Office of Governor Edmund G. Brown Jr., 2017). However, during the national uprisings in 2020, in response to a White Minnesota police officer's killing of George Floyd as well as the long history of police brutality and related injustices against Black Americans, the mainstream green movement (largely comprised of White-led environmental organizations like the Sierra Club, Audubon Society, and others) had a "racial reckoning."

As defenders of Black life pulled down Confederate monuments around the country, the Sierra Club attempted to reckon with the conservation movement's legacy of racism and White supremacy. The first "monument" they started with was John Muir. For example, Muir made derogatory comments about Indigenous peoples, calling them "uncouth" and "savages," largely regarding Indigenous peoples as nonhuman (Nobel, 2016). Other early founders of the Sierra Club were justly scrutinized, such as Joseph LeConte and David Starr Jordan, both of whom were vocal advocates for eugenics and White supremacy. David Starr Jordan was an active member of the American Eugenics Movement and pushed for the sterilization of Indigenous and Black women. Stanford University even requested to rename its building called Jordan Hall (Eugenics at Stanford History Project, 2019). In addition, the Sierra Club stated, "The whiteness and privilege of our early membership fed into a very dangerous idea—one that's still circulating today. The idea is that exploring, enjoying, and protecting the outdoors can be separated from human affairs" (Brune, 2020, para. 7). This is precisely the idea that the Environmental Justice Movement sought to correct, which we will learn more about later in this chapter.

Rethinking John Muir Day

Just as educators committed to social justice and equity have rethought Columbus Day, we also need to rethink John Muir and John Muir Day. The fifth-grade National Park truth detectives got us started thinking about this idea. Below is another lesson for you to engage with, allowing your class to partner with the fifth-grade National Park truth detectives. This lesson will help your students refine their critical questioning skills to enhance their critical consciousness. This is recommended for fourth and fifth grade. However, based on the needs of your class, it can also be modified for different grade levels. This lesson sequence can be implemented over several class periods. The final project, where students create their own memorial, park, or monument, can be modified to take place over several weeks if the teacher wishes to frame it as a project-based learning experience. This lesson plan format is also flexible, and John Muir can be swapped out with other parks and/or people, as seen later in this chapter.

Rethinking John Muir Lesson Plan Idea

So far, we have established a strong foundation for Principle 1: Encourage Student Questions and Observations (Table 3.4). You have also seen in action Element 1: Facilitate Crucial Conversations All Year, and Element 2: Aim to Cultivate and Develop a Critical Consciousness. Next, we will shift the center from John Muir to Dr. J. Drew Lanham, an ecologist, social justice advocate, writer, and MacArthur "genius" who utilizes multiple disciplines. This will showcase Principle 3: In Community with Elders, Activists, and Environmental Professionals, and Element 2: Learning with/from Others.

Table 3.4 Rethinking John Muir Lesson Format

Essential Questions:
- How can individuals and communities shape public memory and influence the public's beliefs and attitudes by creating parks, memorials, and monuments?
- What is the purpose of memorials and monuments? What is their impact on us and how do we think about history?
- What can we learn from parks, memorials, and monuments about the beliefs and values of the people who created them?

Learning Objectives:
- Students will understand that when creating parks, monuments, and memorials, people choose what aspects of a certain history are worth remembering and which parts or which people are intentionally left out.
- Students will understand the connections between history and democracy and how taking an active role in creating and commemorating public spaces can be a form of civic participation.

Frontloading Historical Background Information:
- Have students explore the following resources from PBS, which are all listed in the resources section at the end of this chapter: (1) *The National Parks: America's best idea*; (2) *Photo Gallery. The National Parks: America's best idea*; (3) *The National Parks: A timeline*. This can be done in student groups using devices, in a computer lab, or as a whole-class activity.
- Students can also examine the websites for the following parks and monuments related to John Muir: (1) Muir Redwoods National Monument (U.S. National Park Service); (2) John Muir National Historic Site (U.S. National Park Service)

Discussion Activities:
- Start by having students brainstorm ideas behind the purposes of parks, monuments, and memorials. What purpose do they serve? Who are they for?
- The class can be divided into teams or groups to explore Muir Redwoods National Monument and the John Muir National Historic Site.
- Students can then work in groups and write in their "detective/investigator" notebooks the answers to the following questions:
  → Who is the audience for the park or monument?
  → What is the story or message that the park or monument founder is trying to convey and/or portray to the intended audience? What does the park or monument leave out?
  → What specifically is the park or monument celebrating or recognizing?
- After students work in groups to investigate these questions, the teacher can lead a whole group discussion with these questions:

(Continued)

Table 3.4 (*Continued*)

> - → Why might people want to build parks or monuments?
> - → How does someone's identity impact how they understand or celebrate certain events or people in history? (Refer to the Learning for Justice Social Justice Standards and Domains here.)
> - → Are there consequences of remembering history and people?
> - → Are there consequences for forgetting history? Or erasing history?
> - Students can also break into groups or teams to learn more about the Indigenous lands on which these parks and monuments are located, and the history and governance of the Indigenous peoples.
>
> **Debrief and Discussion (Whole Group or Small Group):**
> - How can recognizing and acknowledging problematic moments or people in history be a form of civic participation?
> - Why is it necessary to acknowledge past injustices to create a more just present and future?
> - Is there any part of our community's local history that is erased or forgotten? Whose perspective is told through parks, memorials, place names, and monuments?
>
> **Final Project–Create Your Own Park, Memorial, or Monument:**
> - Students can work in groups or teams to brainstorm important events in their city, town, or neighborhood's local history. The teacher can narrow this down to specific events, ideas, or individuals that align with the lesson plan. The teacher can also provide students with some appropriate resources for their chosen topic.
> - Students should brainstorm the following questions:
>   - → What important people, events, or ideas are important for us to remember? Why? Has their story been told before? Has their story been erased?
>   - → What message or idea do you want the park or memorial to convey? How does this challenge what we know or do not know about the idea, event, or person?
>   - → How will the park or memorial communicate your ideas? Do you need specific materials, words, shapes, signs, or other elements?
> - Here is an excellent opportunity for multidisciplinary connections. Students can create sketches, prototypes, drawings, paintings, models, and other visual representations. They can utilize educational technology tools such as Google Slides, Google Drawings, and Book Creator, among others.
> - Make sure students put a name and an "artist's statement" on their product. The teacher can have students participate in a "gallery walk" to share ideas, which can be shared with a buddy class or even at a school assembly. There are many possibilities!

Shifting the Center: From John Muir to J. Drew Lanham

A New Kind of Conservationist

In Chapter 1, we learned about Principle 3: In Community with Elders, Activists, and Environmental Professionals. Look at Element 2, Learning with/from Others, and shift the focus from John Muir to center on a new kind of modern-day conservationist and environmentalist. Dr. J. Drew Lanham is a conservationist and a distinguished professor at Clemson University. Utilizing multiple disciplines in his work, he is also a prolific author and poet and is a 2022 MacArthur "genius." His research and teaching focus on forest management of birds. He combines this ecological and scientific knowledge with his lived experiences as a Black man in the U.S. South to explore the intersections of social and environmental justice. A common theme across his writing and poetry is exploring people's historical and cultural connections to the land, particularly for Black Americans, due to the legacy of slavery and Jim Crow segregation. His most notable public works include his 2013 essay, "Nine Rules for the Black Birdwatcher," based on his experiences with threats and stereotypes while birding in the field. These themes are also reflected in his 2017 book *The Home Place: Memoirs of a Colored Man's Love Affair with Nature*. Learning for Justice's Social Justice Standards are also evident in J. Drew Lanham's work. Specifically, look at Table 3.5 for examples of Domain 1: Identity, Domain 3: Justice, and Domain 4: Action.

J. Drew Lanham and the Learning for Justice Social Justice Standards

Now you can see how J. Drew Lanham and his work are aligned with the Learning for Justice Social Justice Standards, particularly Domain 1: Identity, Domain 3: Justice, and Domain 4: Action. Learn more about J. Drew Lanham and his fascinating story! In the spirit of intergenerational learning and collaboration, apply the "3 Steps for Working with Environmental Justice Elders, Activists, and Environmental Professionals." Take a deeper look below!

Step 1: Meet the Environmental Professional and Learn about Their Story

> Meet them virtually through the media or by viewing their website. Build a relationship through literature, see their mission/work, and represent the mission with an artifact they use in their work.

For Step 1, students can learn about J. Drew Lanham's work and mission by watching these two brief videos here: (1) First video: https://www.youtube.com/watch?v=Ox-8tjIhlAc; (2) Second video: https://www.youtube.com/watch?v=8eomGJ5BkYo. Some questions for students to consider after watching the two videos:

Table 3.5 J. Drew Lanham and Learning for Justice's Social Justice Standards

---

Domain 1: Identity (Students Will):
- Recognize that people's intersectional identities interact and create unique and complex ways that people contribute towards the Environmental Movement, environmental justice, and climate justice activism.
- Express pride, confidence, and self-esteem about themselves and their community as environmental justice thinkers and learners.
- Develop historical and cultural knowledge to affirm and describe membership in multiple identity groups and their contributions to the Environmental Justice Movement.
- Recognize the traits of the dominant culture, their own culture, and other cultures, and how to negotiate their identity in multiple spaces.

Domain 3: Justice (Students Will):
- Recognize that stereotypes based on race, gender, class, etc., impact who is considered good at science and capable of working towards environmental justice solutions.
- Environmental justice education and climate justice education can be tools for identifying the inequitable impacts of climate change at the systemic level.

Domain 4: Action (Students Will):
- Plan and carry out collective action using environmental justice as a tool to address larger issues of injustice in the world.
- Make data-informed decisions about how and when to take a stand and make a difference in their community.
- Understand how systems of oppression function in environmental justice and feel empowered with tools to take meaningful steps towards action and change.

- How does J. Drew Lanham use science, art, and writing in his work?
- Why do scientists need to be good writers and communicators?
- What does he mean by "head to heart, science to art?"
- How does he center his lived experiences and his identity in his work? How does this inspire him and influence his work?
- What does he mean by "birds are connected to people and can teach us about issues?"
- What does a student mean when she says, "Color should not define whether you can be in the environment or not?"

Your students can also create biographies of J. Drew Lanham, as he is not typically featured in school libraries. Students can make posters, use Book Creator, or make their own books. Alternatively, even reach J. Drew Lanham with their books! Another possibility is for students to start an environmental justice leaders' section in the classroom or school library to catalog and showcase their learning. Now that we have learned about J. Drew Lanham and his story and work, we will look at Step 2: Join the Mission.

Step 2: Join the Mission

> After young learners have background knowledge of the professionals and their mission/work, they will mimic their work using age-appropriate tools. Students will collect data and use tools like professionals.

J. Drew Lanham has provided a way for the public and students to join his mission in his essay, "9 Rules for the Woke Bird Watcher." The link is here: https://orionmagazine.org/article/9-rules-for-the-woke-birdwatcher/. This poem is accessible to all age groups. J. Drew Lanham outlines nine steps in the essay and depending on the age of the class or the lesson, the teacher can assign different steps to students or utilize the steps to create various projects, assignments, or learning experiences. For example, Step 7 in the 9 Rules for the Woke Birdwatcher is Dismantling Offensive Monuments. The fifth-grade National Park truth detectives have been working towards Step 7. Step 7, Dismantling Offensive Monuments, can also be achieved by implementing the Rethinking John Muir lesson idea, particularly these elements of the lesson sequence:

- Essential Question
- Learning Objectives
- Frontloading Historical Background Information
- Discussion Activities
- Debrief and Discussion

Regarding this step, J. Drew Lanham (2020) states,

> *Dismantle offensive monuments. Watch the golden eagle soar over Mount Rushmore and think of what was stolen, what once rose there, naturally sacred before chisels made men into gods. See the peregrine falcon circling Georgia's Stone Mountain, the world's largest shrine to white supremacy, then imagine that eyesore free of the treasonous rebels marring its granite face. Understand the power of exclusion.*
>
> (para. 7)

Here, Lanham challenges us to challenge the "green status quo" and the "green business as usual," engage in critical questioning, and challenge the actual history embedded in these "green monuments." Lanham bridges the arts and sciences to create a 21st-century conservation model that incorporates social and environmental justice. For our Principles of Environmental Justice for K-5 Students, his work achieves Principle 2: Not Just a Science Issue; his honest multidisciplinary approach achieves Element 1: Engagement and Entry Points across the Curriculum, and Element 2: Environmental Justice Has a History. Time to take a closer look!

J. Drew Lanham challenges us to disrupt the "green status quo" and its historical founders through his fifth rule for the woke birdwatcher:

> *Let history guide you. John Jay Audubon did not care about Black Human lives. Harriet Tubman knew the woods and wetlands well—she even used an owl to identify herself to freedom-seeking souls. Let her be your wild-bird liberty-loving hero.*
>
> (para. 5)

While Harriet Tubman is primarily known as an abolitionist and activist, her knowledge of ecology and the environment was crucial during her work as an Underground Railroad conductor (Weisstuch, 2022), which helped her navigate the landscape and survive. However, this largely remains unknown. This is another National Park truth detector task! Teachers can substitute John Muir in the Rethinking John Muir Lesson Plan sequence and utilize that flexible framework to learn about Harriet Tubman and the Harriet Tubman Underground Railroad National Historic Park in Maryland.

Now that students have had opportunities to learn about J. Drew Lanham's work and mission and have engaged in age-appropriate activities to learn the skills and tools utilized by the environmental professional, Step 3: Extend the mission and take civic action! Take a look below.

Step 3: Extend the Mission and Take Civic Action

> Once young learners have built the professional's skill set in Step 2, they will synthesize that skill into their mission to take civic action. This mission can expand on the work that the professional is already doing or take on a new mission inspired by the professional's work and what the student is passionate about.

In Step 3, one idea is to have students complete the final project in the John Muir Lesson Plan Sequence, which tasks students with creating their park, memorial, or monument. Students can critique who we have historically positioned as environmental heroes and investigate unsung environmental heroes and conservationists in their local community, and unknown environmental heroes throughout history, such as Harriet Tubman. Students can also use the other 9 Rules of the Woke Birdwatcher for project inspiration, such as renaming birds named after problematic historical figures. For example, Rule 4: "Be bold. Speak up. Identify racism as you would call out a crow among snow buntings. Silence lets the oppression grow unchecked."

Lesson Idea: Creating Upstander Superheroes and Social Justice Birdwatchers
For example, students can learn what it means to be an "upstander" by watching this video from Facing History and Ourselves: https://www.facinghistory.org/why-facing-history/choosing-participate. Students can create upstander characters, upstander superheroes, and the anatomy of a social justice birdwatcher. To integrate art like J. Drew Lanham does in his work, students can sketch, paint, or draw their figures or characters. Students can also integrate writing, as J. Drew Lanham does, by writing stories or books about their characters. Students can also incorporate digital literacy by creating infographics or posters using Canva or Google Slides, or by designing a book in Book Creator. Some ideas are below, and students can be creative and have their characters have several different body parts or multiple body parts:

- Head: What does the character think
- Eyes: What does the character see
- Ears: What the character hears
- Mouth: What does the character say
- Torso (heart): What does the character feel or believe
- Arms and hands: What does the character do
- Legs and feet: What is the character doing, or what do they want to happen

Students can share their upstander superheroes and social justice birdwatchers with a buddy class, a school assembly, the principal, families, or even J. Drew Lanham!

Also, as elementary school teachers and educators committed to equity and social justice, you are primed to teach about environmental justice and climate justice because they are not just science topics. Elementary teachers teach multiple subjects and possess a unique skill set to help students make critical connections across disciplines, subjects, and content standards. As we progress through the book, there will be even more ways to think critically and act on disrupting the "green status quo" and "green business as usual." To reflect on what you learned in this first section, consider the following reflection questions about your professional practice.

In this chapter, we have worked on Principle 1: Encourage Student Questions and Observations, Element 1: Facilitate Crucial Conversations All Year, and Element 2: Aim to Cultivate and Develop a Critical Consciousness. We have shifted the center, challenged the "green status quo," and moved from John Muir to modern-day conservationists, social justice, and environmental justice advocates like Dr. J. Drew Lanham. We have also learned that J. Drew Lanham's work strongly aligns with Learning for Justice's Social Justice Standards, particularly in Domain 1: Identity, Domain 3: Justice, and Domain 4: Action. As elementary school teachers, we are well-equipped to teach about environmental and climate justice because they encompass more than just science topics. We have also seen how J. Drew Lanham's work aligns with Principle 2: Not Just a Science Issue, specifically Element 1: Engagement and Entry Points across the Curriculum, and Element 2: Environmental Justice Has a History. In the next chapter, we will continue our exploration of these themes, particularly by learning about a concept called intersectionality and how this will help us move towards intersectional environmental justice. This will help with the connection between "head and heart" that J. Drew Lanham discusses in his work and one of the videos. Before moving on, do not forget to check out the reflection questions for professional practice and the Further Reading section for resources for students and teachers from this chapter. They are listed below!

 **Reflection Questions for Professional Practice**

Chapter 3 Questions
- What are some other ways to rethink Earth Day?
- What are some other ways that you can rethink John Muir Day? Who are some local environmental leaders in your community? Who are the unheard voices? What are the untold narratives?
- J. Drew Lanham talks about "head to heart, science to art" as part of his professional practice as a conservationist and social justice advocate. What are some ways that you can integrate this concept into your classroom?
- What are other ways students can be "upstanders" and respond to injustices?

Further Reading: Resources for Teachers and Students

Videos and Resources for Teachers

Grist. *How can we make national parks accessible to everybody?* https://www.youtube.com/watch?v=-zdA33hhpbQ&t=19s

PBS. *Photo Gallery. The National Parks: America's best idea.* https://www.pbs.org/kenburns/the-national-parks/photo-gallery

PBS. *The National Parks: A timeline.* https://www.pbs.org/kenburns/the-national-parks/timeline

PBS. *The National Parks: America's best idea.* https://www.pbs.org/kenburns/the-national-parks/

SubjectToClimate. *ELA lesson: Connotations in nature writing.* https://subjecttoclimate.org/lesson-plans/ela-lesson-connotation-in-nature-writing

SubjectToClimate. *Nature and the self poetry lesson.* https://subjecttoclimate.org/lesson-plans/nature-and-the-self-poetry-lesson

SubjectToClimate. *Nature walk poetry activity.* https://subjecttoclimate.org/lesson-plans/nature-walk-poetry-activity

The Atlantic. *The experiment podcast: The problem with America's National Parks.* https://podcasts.apple.com/us/podcast/the-experiment/id1549704404

Books for Teachers

Cooper, C. (2023). *Better living through birding: Notes from a Black man in the natural world.* New York, NY: Random House Large Print.

Klein, N. (2014). *This changes everything: Capitalism vs. the climate.* New York, NY: Simon & Schuster

Lanham, J. D. (2013, October 23). Nine rules for the Black birdwatcher. Great Barrington, MA: *Orion Magazine.* https://orionmagazine.org/article/9-rules-for-the-black-birdwatcher/

Lanham, J. D. (2017). *The home place: Memoirs of a colored man's love affair with nature.* Minneapolis, MN: Milkweed Editions.

Lanham, J. D. (2020, December 3). Nine rules for the woke birdwatcher. Great Barrington, MA: *Orion Magazine.* https://orionmagazine.org/article/9-rules-for-the-woke-birdwatcher/

Lanham J. D. (2021). *Sparrow envy: Field guide to birds and lesser beasts.* Spartangurg, SC: Hub City Press.

Lanham, J. D. (2024). *Joy is the justice we give ourselves.* Spartangurg, SC: Hub City Press.

Lanham, J. D., & Kendler, J. (2023). *Dear Earth: Art and hope in a time of crisis.* London: Hayward Gallery Publishing.

Larson, K. C. (2024). *Bound for the promised land: Harriet Tubman: Portrait of an American hero.* New York, NY: Penguin Random House.

Picture Books for Students

Ahuja, N., & Syed, A. (2021). *Rise up and write it: With real mail, posters, and more!* New York, NY: HarperFestival.

Barretta, G., & Morrison, F. (2020). *The secret garden of George Washington Carver.* New York, NY: Tegan Books.

Benford. H. (2025). *Ridhma Pandey biography for curious kids: Youth activist for environmental justice.* Independently Published.

Benford. H. (2025). *Xiuhtezcatl Martinez biography for curious kids: Environmental activist and Indigenous rights advocate.* Independently Published.

Hillery, T. (2020). *Harlem grown: How one big idea transformed a neighborhood.* New York, NY: Simon & Schuster/Paula Wiseman Books.

Tariq, A. (2021). *Fatima's great outdoors.* New York, NY: Kokila

References

Brune, M. (2020). *Pulling down our monuments.* Sierra Club. https://www.sierraclub.org/michael-brune/2020/07/john-muir-early-history-sierra-club

Eugenics at Stanford History Project. (2019, February 16). *Request to rename Jordan Hall.* https://1e033807-0690-4644-9331-5b6e588f7c1e.filesusr.com/ugd/124541_b0231655bdfc46f9bada4df5f21e0a06.pdf

Learning for Justice. (2022). *Social justice standards.* https://www.learningforjustice.org/frameworks/social-justice-standards

Nobel, J. (2016, July 26). *The miseducation of John Muir: A close examination of the wilderness icon's early travels reveals a deep love for trees, and some ugly feelings about people.* Atlas Obscura. https://www.atlasobscura.com/articles/the-miseducation-of-john-muir

Office of Governor Edmund G. Brown Jr. (2017, April 21). *Governor Brown issues proclamation declaring John Muir Day.* https://archive.gov.ca.gov/archive/gov39/2017/04/21/news19759/index.html

United States Senate. (n.d). *Gaylor Nelson promotes the first Earth Day.* https://www.senate.gov/artandhistory/history/minute/Gaylord_Nelson_Promotes_the_First_Earth_Day.htm

Weisstuch, L. (2022, March 21). Harriet Tubman is famous for being an abolitionist and political activist, but she was also a naturalist. *Smithsonian Magazine.* https://www.smithsonianmag.com/history/harriet-tubman-is-famous-for-being-an-abolitionist-and-political-activist-but-she-was-also-a-naturalist-180979689/

4

Towards an Intersectional Environmental Justice

Spotlight: Fourth-Grade Natural Disaster Analysts

Mrs. Kahale played a few keys on her piano to get the attention of the fourth graders. She could feel the excitement in the air. The energy and the conversation seemed to be focused on two specific boys and what they were saying. Sigh…She knew immediately who they were…

The rest of the class recognized the attention-getter and stopped talking, but Miguel and Fernando just kept going. All eyes turned to them. Miguel noticed and blushed, and said, "Sorry, Mrs. Kahale." Fernando said, "Hey, Mrs. Kahale. Miguel told me that his sister is learning about Bad Bunny in college for one of his classes! I was like, 'No way, that's not for college!' Whachu think, Mrs. Kahale?"

The rest of the class turned and started to make comments to each other upon hearing about Bad Bunny. Chatter quickly filled the room! "My tia always listens to Bad Bunny when cleaning the house," said Tara. "I saw him on YouTube," said Luis. "Estamos bien," said Alejandro, "I love that song!"

Mrs. Kahale said, "Oh yes, I saw that on the news! At Loyola Marymount University, there is a class on Bad Bunny. Miguel, I know your sister is going to college in Los Angeles. Does she go to that university?"

"Yeah," said Miguel. I forgot the name of the college, but that's all. It has three letters: LMU.

Mrs. Kahale said,

DOI: 10.4324/9781003620709-7

Wow, Miguel, that sounds like a great class. Your sister is so lucky! Bad Bunny is very famous indeed. He is breaking many records on the Billboard lists right now. He is the first Latin artist to log 100 entries on the Billboard Hot 100 list!

"Ohhhhhhhhhhhh!" the class exclaimed! Mrs. Kahale said, "I can tell that you're all super excited about this."

"Great," said Mrs. Kahale.

Hmmmm…this gives me an idea…Okay, class, we have been learning about natural disasters in science. Today, we will learn about Hurricane Maria, which impacted Puerto Rico in September 2017. Speaking of Bad Bunny, in his first TV performance in 2018, he dedicated it to Puerto Rico, as he did not want people to forget about the victims of the natural disaster. He came out with a new song called "Una Velita" (a little candle) last year, which was seven years after Hurricane Maria. We will learn more about why people and the world forgot about Puerto Rico and why Bad Bunny is using his global platform as a form of activism to draw attention to this injustice.

"Remember, to investigate the truth all year and across all of our subjects, we are learning about the three components of critical consciousness." Mrs. Kahale pointed to a poster on the wall that had a pie chart depicting the three components of critical consciousness: (1) Social analysis, (2) Political agency, and (3) Social action.

"Today we are going to work on our social analysis," she said. Several heads bobbed up and down in recognition. "First, we will watch a video of a student your age in Puerto Rico (listed in the resources section at the end of this chapter). The student will share her experience after Hurricane Maria. Next, we are going to watch a report from Democracy Now about some of the injustices the Puerto Ricans experienced after the hurricane."

Mrs. Kahale said,

I also have a question: How long after a natural disaster should people wait for essential items like clean water, food, and electricity? Think for a minute and then show me a thumb on your chin when you have your answer.

"Like 1 day," said Rosa. "24 hours," said Michael. "No, like right away! IMM-MEDIATELY!" said Peter, for extra emphasis.

"You are all correct; you would think that is what the response would be," said Mrs. Kahale. "Well, for the people in Puerto Rico, nearly two weeks after the Hurricane devastated the island, the people in the capital were facing shortages of food, water, and electricity."

"WHAT? TWO WEEKS!!!" *said Jose. Flabbergasted, he threw his hands up in the air for effect.*

Mrs. Kahale nodded her head. "Indeed...that is an authentic reaction, Jose. I think that is what many of us are feeling. It is actually worse than that. After the Hurricane, Puerto Rico experienced the longest blackout in U.S. history, which lasted 11 months."

"WHAT!!!!!" *said Jose, who hit his forehead with his palm.* "That is insane!" *said Charlotte. The rest of the class had their mouths hanging wide open in shock.* "No wonder Bad Bunny thinks everyone forgot, cuz they did, THEY DID!" *exclaimed Jose.*

"Bad Bunny, he has that social analysis!" *shouted Jimena.*

"Yeah, and Bad Bunny knows he is really famous, and people listen to him because he got all those awards, lists, and stuff," *said Mark.* "That is the political agency, he knows he can make a change because he is famous and stuff," *said Mark with a nod of his head.*

"Does he do any social action?" *said De'Shawn.* "Maybe he wants us to do social action! Or like America or the rest of the world!" *exclaimed Bryan.*

"Wow! Excellent thinking, everyone. I am so impressed!" *Mrs. Kahale said,* "This brings us to our essential question: Who is responsible for Puerto Rico's recovery from the devastation of Hurricane Maria?"

Mrs. Kahale has set up a great backdrop for many lessons about Hurricane Maria. For example, students can expand upon this established frontloading in a few different ways:

- *Learn about Puerto Rico's history and what it means to be a U.S. territory*
- *Use the read-aloud book, "Alicia and the Hurricane / Alicia Y El Huracán: A Story of Puerto Rico / Un Cuento de Puerto Rico." A video is here: https://youtu.be/pNjOjzWOpeQ?feature=shared*
- *Interviewed Puerto Ricans who lived through Hurricane Maria for their perspectives in an oral history format. An example from the University of Oregon is here: https://blogs.uoregon.edu/theuopuertoricoproject/*
- *Students can research the U.S. response to natural disasters in U.S. states vs. U.S. territories. Students can study the media coverage, the type of aid provided, the amount of aid provided, and the perspectives of local people.*
- *Students can debate or role-play who is responsible for ensuring that locals can rebuild in Puerto Rico after Hurricane Maria. Students will justify their arguments with primary source documents and facts.*
- *Students can investigate/research: How might the fact that the residents of Puerto Rico cannot vote for the President of the United States affect the government's response?*

- *Students can engage in a writing activity where they write a report to Congress or the President, outlining the type of aid Puerto Ricans need. Now and in the future. Students can use primary source documents, images, videos, or other media to support their arguments and writing.*
- *Students can also research Bad Bunny's activism regarding Hurricane Maria and create books about him using BookCreator.*
- *Teachers can use Teaching for Change's Resource Caribbean Connections: Puerto Rico, which introduces students to the history, economics, environment, and culture of Puerto Rico through essays, poetry, and fiction. https://www.teachingforchange.org/books/puerto-rico*
- *Students can debate whether the response to Hurricane Maria is environmental racism and compare it to other natural disaster responses (i.e., Hurricane Katrina).*

Now that we have seen an example from the fourth-grade natural disaster analysts, we must examine some key takeaways. The entry point was a pop-culture reference to the musical artist Bad Bunny, which the students found exciting. I have found that knowing "kid culture" is something really useful, or becoming attuned to what students are interested in. This provides a great piggy bank for lesson ideas to captivate student interest! Likewise, Mrs. Kahale heard a student's conversation and invited students to share with the class. She then made a connection to what students had been studying in their science lesson about natural disasters. Through this pop-culture entry, Mrs. Kahale was addressing Principle 1: Encourage Student Questions and Observations and Element 1: Facilitate Crucial Conversations All Year. She also pointed out that musicians can use their platform to raise awareness about social justice and environmental justice issues, which we will cover in this chapter.

To address Element 2: Cultivate and Develop a Critical Consciousness, Mrs. Kahale built upon her established best practice of using a poster in her classroom that outlined the three components of critical consciousness and referring students back to that language. She also emphasized how Bad Bunny was using his platform to raise awareness about Hurricane Maria in the American consciousness. Since students were already familiar with this language, they were able to recognize these elements in someone else, and the class analyzed how Bad Bunny was engaging with the three aspects of critical consciousness. Mrs. Kahale then posed the guiding question: How long after a natural disaster should people wait for essential items like clean water, food, and electricity? From here, the teacher can take this lesson in a few different directions, some of which are listed at the end of the vignette.

For example, for younger students, there is a read-aloud of a bilingual picture book that provides background information and addresses core speaking and listening standards. Students can also make connections to an English Language Arts lesson by listening to oral histories of Puerto Ricans after Hurricane Maria, which was started by a class at the University of Oregon. If there is a Puerto Rican community in your school's town or city, students can also invite local community members or family members to come to the class to share Puerto Rican history and culture. Students can create original oral history books with Book Creator or Google Slides and share them with the school library or school community. For connections to social studies, students can examine what it means to be a U.S. territory and how that impacts natural disaster relief. Alternatively, utilize Teaching Change's resource, "Caribbean Connections: Puerto Rico," to learn more about the history, culture, economy, and environment of Puerto Rico. As you can see, many disciplinary curricular entry points are modifiable for different grade levels and student abilities. Now that we have unpacked the key takeaways from the awesome fourth-grade natural disaster analysts, let us learn more about "intersectionality" and why it is so important when teaching for/about environmental justice.

Intersectionality: A Brief Primer

What Is Intersectionality and Intersectional Theory?

Let us explore why "intersectionality" is a crucial concept for educators, particularly in the context of social justice and equity. Let us start with the person who "coined" this term. Do you know who that is? It is Kimberlé Crenshaw, a legal scholar who studies civil rights, critical race theory, Black feminist legal theory, and the intersection of racism and the law. She holds positions at Columbia University Law School and the University of California, Los Angeles School of Law. In 1989, Crenshaw coined the concept and analytic tool known as "intersectionality," which is rooted in her experiences as both a Black woman. This tool was developed to describe how individual characteristics, such as race, gender, class, etc., intersect with each other to overlap and subsequently create different levels of oppression and privilege. Over time, intersectionality has been used to include the intersectional identities of other historically and contemporarily marginalized groups and to consider other factors like sexual orientation and non-binary and trans identities. However, it is essential not to overlook the contributions of Black women to this foundational scholarship. If you would like to learn more, a video about intersectionality is listed in the resources section at the end of this chapter. Let's take a second look at the Learning for Justice Social Justice Standards to examine how intersectionality plays a role in this. Especially Domain 1: Identity. We will grade-level outcomes and scenarios, and learn why this is for educators committed to justice and equity.

Why This Matters: Why You Cannot Teach about the Environment without Intersectionality

Domain 1: Identity

In Domain 1: Identity, teachers provide students with opportunities to learn about their origins and their identities. The intention behind this is to reduce bias as students learn about their privileges, responsibilities, and identities. The overarching goal is to develop positive social identities and understand how these multiple identities overlap and intersect to create multi-dimensional individuals. To learn from the diverse narratives about our planet, it is important to validate and honor all students' lived experiences. As I unfortunately experienced in my schooling, not all students' environmental knowledge is seen as valuable in our dominant education system, as the environmental movement has been predominantly White. In addition, to

Table 4.1 Grades K-2

Anchor Standard	Grade-Level Outcome	Environmental Justice Teaching Ideas and Resources
Identity 2	I can talk about interesting and healthy ways that some people who share my group identities live their environmental lives.	• Ambreen Tariq's picture book, *Fatima's Great Outdoors*, tells the story of an immigrant family in the Midwest who go on their first camping trip. • *Harlem Grown*, a picture book by Tony Hillery, tells the story of a garden in New York City that grew out of an abandoned lot and feeds a neighborhood. • *Jayden's Impossible Garden*, a picture book by Melina Mangal, tells the story of seeing nature in urban environments and how intergenerational collaboration brings a community garden to life. • *This is How We Play: A Celebration of Disability and Adaptation*, a picture book by disability activist Jessica Slice, tells the story of how people with disabilities and their families play.

Table 4.2 Grades 3–5

Anchor Standard	Grade-Level Outcome	Environmental Justice Teaching Ideas and Resources
ID.3–5.3	I know that all my group identities are part of who I am, but none of them fully describe me, and this is true for other people, too	• *IntersectionAllies: We Make Room for All*, by Chelsea Johnson and LaToya Council, provides a kid-friendly introduction to intersectional feminism. • *Julián Is a Mermaid*, by Jessica Love, is a Stonewall Book Award Winner and tells the story of a child who dresses up as a mermaid. • *Buzzing with Questions: The Inquisitive Mind of Charles Henry Turner*, by Janice N. Harrington, is a story about the first Black entomologist. • *Where is Rodney*, by Rebecca Lehr, is a picture book about Rodney, a boy with disabilities who struggles inside the classroom but thrives when outdoors.

add intersectionality, other people are often excluded from the environmental space due to ability/disability, not knowing how to "do" outdoor activities that are culturally constructed, like camping, or even having inequitable access to nature. Here are some ideas adapted from the Learning for Justice Social Justice Standards for incorporating intersectionality into your classroom instruction, specifically as it pertains to environmental justice and environmental education. There are different examples by grade band: K-2 and 3–5 (Tables 4.1 and 4.2).

Additionally, many identity-focused conservation and environmental affinity groups center on the concept of intersectionality. Here are some examples to explore below. A lot of these national organizations listed have state chapters and regional chapters. Can you find a chapter in your area?

- *Outdoor Asian*: An organization seeking to build a diverse and inclusive community of Asian Americans and Pacific Islanders in outdoor spaces. Website: https://www.outdoorasian.com/
- *Latino Outdoors*: An organization that seeks to inspire, connect, and engage Latino communities in the outdoors and embrace *cultura y familia* as part of the outdoor narrative, ensuring our history, heritage, and leadership are valued and represented. Website: https://latinooutdoors.org/

- *Outdoor Afro*: Celebrates and inspires Black connections and leadership in nature. Our national not-for-profit organization reconnects Black people to our lands, water, and wildlife through outdoor education, recreation, and conservation. Website: https://outdoorafro.org
- *Indigenous Environmental Network*: An alliance of Indigenous Peoples whose shared mission is to protect the sacredness of Earth Mother from contamination and exploitation. Website: https://www.ienearth.org/
- *Indigenous Climate Action*: An Indigenous-led organization guided by a diverse group of Indigenous knowledge keepers, water protectors, and land defenders from communities and regions across the country. https://www.indigenousclimateaction.com/
- *The Venture Out Project*: Leads backpacking and wilderness trips for the queer and transgender community. They also conduct transgender inclusion workshops. Website: https://www.ventureoutproject.com/aota
- *Feminist Bird Club*: Dedicated to promoting inclusivity in birding while fundraising and providing a safe opportunity for members of the LGBTQIA+ community. Website: https://www.feministbirdclub.org/

Community-Centered and Intersectional Approaches

After reading about and exploring the identity-focused conservation and environmental affinity groups that center intersectionality, you may be wondering what this looks like at the community level. How do these organizations help local communities tackle environmental injustice, particularly in frontline communities? Time to examine some community-based organizations that incorporate intersectionality into their approaches to achieving environmental justice. Explore Tables 4.3–4.5 for examples of case studies that feature community-centered approaches to addressing environmental and climate justice around the country. Three states and three specific issues of environmental injustice are in focus: (1) Hawai'i: Land Conservation; (2) New York: Healthy Homes; and (3) California: Standing Up to Big Polluters. There is also a breakdown in each table of how the organization addresses and utilizes the concept of intersectionality in its work. Can you think of similar organizations in your community that also center intersectionality in their approaches? Why is this important?

Some ideas for implementation in your classroom include having students investigate the issues that the organizations are trying to address, such

Table 4.3 Hawai'i: Land Conservation (Organization: Mālama Pu'uloa)

Location	Hawai'i
Environmental Injustices Addressed	The Pearl Harbor area was once a vibrant ecosystem that served the needs of many local Hawaiian families, plants, animals, and diverse economies, as well as various ways of life. However, a changing climate, overuse from population increases, military presence, and growing tourism exposure have all negatively altered the native ecosystem.
Assisting Organization	Mālama Pu'uloa engages the community by educating local youth through land-based programs and creating partnerships to support collaborative goals. The Hawaiian concept of "mālama" means to take care of, tend to, attend to, care for, preserve, and protect. This tradition is centered on all project partners. To date, Mālama Pu'uloa has engaged over 20,000 community volunteers (including 40 K college schools) to restore nearly 15 acres from invasive mangroves, re-establish traditional food systems, and create a growing network of community members united in purpose.
Organization Resources	Organization Website: https://www.hepfreehawaii.org/news/welcome-malama-puuloa Mālama Pu'uloa Island Life Video: https://www.youtube.com/watch?v=ZHdg99T9TzQ ArcGIS StoryMap: The Pu'uloa Strategic Partnership: https://storymaps.arcgis.com/stories/0beb13c4c833420f87eeda3e65b2cdc5
Intersectionality	Race, socioeconomic status, and language

as land conservation, Healthy Homes, and Standing Up to Big Polluters. For example, how do these environmental injustices play out in your local town or community? Are there organizations that are working to address this issue? Are the organizations in your regional city or community attending to intersectionality and community-centered approaches in their work? Students can also research these issues in their community and create their own visions and ideas for potential solutions and approaches. For example, students could write letters to their local representatives, invite community members to serve as guest speakers, or contact the city mayor. Now that you have learned more about intersectionality, we will explore how analytic tools are essential when teaching about environmental justice and climate justice.

Table 4.4 New York: Healthy Homes (Organization: We Act for Environmental Justice)

Location	New York
Environmental Injustices Addressed	Over two-thirds of New York City residents rent their homes, and this rate is even higher among low-income residents. A lack of affordable housing options in New York City, particularly due to gentrification, presents significant challenges for low- and middle-income families. Low-quality housing and old buildings mean that landlords do not always properly repair pre-existing housing deficiencies, such as cracks, mold, pests, and lead-based peeling paint within the home—all of which can lead to health disparities, including high rates of childhood asthma, lead exposure, or poisoning.
Assisting Organization	We Act for Environmental Justice's mission is to build healthy communities by ensuring that people of color and/or low-income residents participate meaningfully in the creation of sound and fair environmental health and protection policies and practices.
Organization Resources	We Act for Environmental Justice: https://www.weact.org/ We Act for Environmental Justice Healthy Homes: https://www.weact.org/whatwedo/areasofwork/healthy-homes/ NYC Lead Outreach Campaign: https://www.weact.org/campaigns/nyc-lead-outreach-campaign/ Coalition for Asthma Free Homes: https://www.weact.org/campaigns/cafh/
Intersectionality	Race, socioeconomic status

Towards an Intersectional Environmentalism: Liberation for People + Planet

The first intersections we will explore are those of socioeconomics and race. We learned about the Yale Program on Climate Change Communication's Six Americas in the previous chapter. The overall significance is that the audiences most worried about climate change (approximately 56% alarmed or concerned) are also the most likely to be supportive of goals to advance climate justice. Thus, there is substantial evidence in support of climate justice. However, despite high levels of support, awareness remains low. Most Alarmed and Concerned people recognize and acknowledge that climate change disproportionately impacts people based on socioeconomic status and race. Let us learn more.

Table 4.5 California: Standing up to Big Polluters (Organization: Asian Pacific Environmental Network)

Location	California
Environmental Injustices Addressed	Oil fields, fracking wells, industrial agriculture, coal mines, dirty power plants, industrial freight, or massive refineries: The fossil fuel economy is poisoning the air we breathe, the water we drink, the land that we grow food on, and the people we love. The Asian Pacific Environmental Network (APEN) builds the power of Asian communities on the frontlines to stop big polluters from poisoning our families and destabilizing our climate.
Assisting Organization	The APEN builds the power of Asian communities on the frontlines to stop big polluters from poisoning our families and destabilizing our climate. APEN is actively fighting to stop Chevron from expanding its massive oil refinery in Richmond and organizing to stop major developers from transporting dirty coal through the Bay.
Organization Resources	Asian Pacific Environmental Network: https://apen4ej.org/ Lipo and Saeng's Story: https://vimeo.com/364407516 Pan Hai Bo's Story: https://vimeo.com/364407591
Intersectionality	Race, socioeconomic status, immigration status/citizenship, language

Socioeconomics and Race

Time to learn from a former teacher who is a "genius!" Catherine Coleman Flowers is "an environmental and climate justice activist bringing attention to the largely invisible problem of inadequate waste and water sanitation infrastructure in rural communities in the United States" (Catherine Coleman Flowers, n.d.). Her orientation to activism began in childhood in Lowndes County, Alabama. The daughter of civil rights activists, her parents taught Coleman Flowers "that to be a good neighbor meant to be actively involved in making the community a better place to live for all" (Stone & McClellan, 2024, para. 1). After she served in the military and was a high school social studies teacher (how cool is that), she founded the Center for Rural Enterprise and Environmental Justice. Among her many notable accomplishments: A 2020 MacArthur "genius," Vice Chair of the White House Environmental Justice Advisory Council, one of TIME's 100 most influential people in the world, and one of Forbes' 50 over 50. Impressive!

One of the things we take for granted is sanitation. If you live in the United States, this may be something that you do not consider. Access to sanitation may also be framed as a "third-world problem" that exists "over there" and is far removed from our daily concerns. Did you know that sanitation access is racialized in the United States? In Coleman Flowers' research, she found that a majority of residents in Lowndes County, Alabama, live without a properly working and basic sanitation infrastructure. Another discovery was that sanitation inequities in the United States are racialized due to systemic racism's impacts on housing availability, public health enforcement and policies, and land tenure. Thus, sanitation is a "human rights issue" (Winkler & Flowers, 2017) and also America's "dirty secret" (Flowers, 2020). Coleman Flowers reflects on the influential teachers in her life and describes Al Gore's 2006 film, *An Inconvenient Truth,* as a pivotal learning experience, during which she made connections between economic development, infrastructure, wastewater, and climate change. She states:

> *The film really brought it all home for me—and made clear the connection between why climate change was happening, why we were having wastewater problems in Lowndes County, and how those problems were contributing to a rise in diseases that we thought we had gotten rid of. It was because it was getting warmer, and these tropical illnesses that we thought would happen in other places, in other climates, could actually manifest here in the United States. That is how I got involved and what ultimately brought me to where I am now.*
> (Stone & McClellan, 2024, para. 5)

For more from Catherine Coleman Flowers, listen to this podcast episode below. In the podcast, she explains why environmental injustices often criminalize poverty and perpetually penalize and exploit poor people, thus making rural Americans more vulnerable to environmental injustice and environmental racism: https://podcasts.apple.com/us/podcast/catherine-coleman-flowers-when-listening-becomes-activism/id1459675744?i=1000520584812.

From Coleman Flowers' work, we can also clearly see that socioeconomics and race intersect to create inequitable access to sanitation in the United States. This is not only an environmental justice issue, but it is also a clear example of environmental racism. In addition, while most Alarmed and Concerned people recognize and acknowledge that climate change disproportionately impacts people based on socioeconomics and race, there is even less awareness that gender is also a determining factor for disproportionately experiencing the impacts of climate change. Let us explore why this is the case and what it means for us as teachers committed to social justice and equity.

Climate Change and Gender

Rural Women

Did you know that climate change has disproportionately affected girls and women worldwide? The International Panel on Climate Change (IPCC) found that climate-related dangers further exaggerate existing gender inequalities. According to Verona Callantes, an intergovernmental specialist with UN Women, climate-related hazards cause "higher workloads for women, occupational hazards indoors and outdoors, psychological and emotional stress, and higher mortality compared to men" (McCarthy, 2020). Climate change is also a "threat magnifier," meaning it exacerbates the existing social, political, and economic tensions that often exist in conflict-affected environments. This means that paying attention to intersectionality is important, as the intersections of gender, socioeconomics, and race make specific groups of women more vulnerable to climate impacts.

How do you get food for yourself or your family? You can go to the local grocery store, farmers' market, or supermarket. However, what if you had to walk long distances for your food? What if you had to walk these long distances alone? Would it be safe? Rural women around the world are severely impacted because they bear a disproportionate responsibility for obtaining fuel, water, and food. Women also have to travel farther to get the resources that they need for their families. Consequently, if rural women are forced to travel farther distances alone, they are more vulnerable to encountering gender-based violence like sexual assault on their journey.

Earlier, we learned about Catherine Coleman Flowers, who is advocating for environmental justice in rural Black communities in the United States. Rural people (especially women) and their increased vulnerability to climate change are practically invisible in our national climate plans! The Food and Agriculture Organization of the United Nations (FAO) (2024) found that in the 24 countries analyzed for the report, only 6% of the 4,164 climate actions proposed mention women, 2% explicitly mention youths, and less than 1% mention poor and rural populations. Don't you think that agricultural policies are missing a timely opportunity to address not only gender inequality but socioeconomic inequality? This demonstrates that intersectionality is necessary to fully comprehend how various social factors, such as race, gender, and socioeconomic status, intersect to amplify environmental impacts disproportionately. To learn more about why rural women pay the highest price in the climate crisis, listen to this podcast below: https://soundcloud.com/unfao/fao-talks-phillips-gender-climate?utm_source=clipboard&utm_campaign=wt-share&utm_medium=widget&utm_content=https%253A%252F%252Fsoundcloud.com%252Funfao%252Ffao-talks-phillips-gender-climate.

Indigenous Women

In Chapter 3, the fifth-grade National Park truth detectives accurately recognized that Indigenous peoples are the original stewards and caretakers of the land. Thus, while climate change disproportionately impacts the rural poor and rural women, Indigenous women are also disproportionately affected due to the combined impacts of both gender inequities and settler colonialism. Canadian researchers Chapola et al. (2024) found that Indigenous communities, such as the Métis, Cree, and First Nations, in Western Canada possess rich cultural traditions deeply intertwined with the land. As the fifth-grade National Park truth detectives reminded us, Indigenous communities are closely connected to the land and rely on the land for cultural practices, spiritual identity, and physical sustenance. Thus, climate change brings extreme weather and a loss of traditional lands and natural resources.

How would you feel if your heritage, culture, and livelihood were threatened? I am sure you would feel extremely anxious and unsettled! Thus, Indigenous women are more prone to mental health challenges due to climate change. The Truth and Reconciliation Commission of Canada recognizes that any efforts towards reconciliation and healing must center on Indigenous-led initiatives. Ultimately, this calls for not only "Land Back" but "rematriation" of the land. Rematriation is led by Indigenous women and is meant to counter patriarchal systems and return to matrilineal societies and matriarchal ways of knowing. You can learn more about the Land Back movement by exploring the resources available at https://ndncollective.org/landback/ and https://landback.org/.

Do you have an electric vehicle? Are there buildings in your town that have solar panels? We typically think of these "green" products as beneficial for the environment, but have you considered where they come from or how they are made? Furthermore, who is affected by their existence? It was found that climate change disproportionately impacts Indigenous women in Peru (Moulton & Carey, 2023). This is due to the legacy of colonization and the demand for natural resources that people in the global North need for gadgets such as electric vehicles and solar panels. This demand for resources to fuel the "green economy" or the "just transition" consequently results in a "double exposure" for Indigenous women in Peru. Wonder why that is? Let us learn more!

A Just and Green Transition for Whom?

According to studies by the Peruvian Ministry of Environment (MINAM) and Amnesty International, Indigenous women are highly susceptible to the health impacts of mining and heavy metal byproducts like lead, arsenic, and mercury. Did you know that Peru is the world's second-largest copper producer? Peruvian copper is utilized in electric vehicles, wind turbines, and solar panels, thereby contributing to the transition away from fossil fuels. However, Quechua women in Indigenous communities like Chuicuni in the Peruvian Andes said that near the MMG Limited Las Bambas viper mine, hundreds of trucks pass by their homes and cover their pastures and gardens with pollution, which kills their livestock and stunts their children's growth. Doesn't this injustice sound familiar? This sounds similar to the concerns of environmental justice leaders in the United States, who are fighting against landfills and toxic waste dumps located near homes and schools in frontline communities. As we can see, environmental injustice and environmental racism have a global context. We are going to continue learning about this in future chapters.

Thus, international representatives from 35 countries at the Conference on Indigenous Peoples and the Just Transition released a statement that said, "the current trajectory of the energy transition fails to meet the criteria of justice," especially for Indigenous communities and especially Indigenous women at the frontlines of the climate crisis (Moulton, 2024). As educators committed to social justice and equity, we recognize that we must also teach a community's resistance, not just the narrative of their oppression. Women in Peru are fighting back and resisting mining!

Melania Canales Poma, the former president of the largest Peruvian Indigenous women's organization, says that by resisting mining, Indigenous women are safeguarding all lives, as

> *Indigenous women defend life, all life…and therefore demand territorial sovereignty and legal security of Indigenous rights to maintain their self-stated role as "guardians of Pachamama [Mother Earth]" that allow them to make claims to territory that differ from other historically marginalized communities.*
>
> (Moulton, 2024, para. 3)

This ultimately presents an opportunity to go beyond just gender, and instead center Indigenous and intersectional climate and environmental justice. This is what Gen-Z is focusing on in their environmental justice and climate justice activism. We will learn more later in this chapter! Thus, while climate change and environmental injustices do indeed disproportionately impact women and girls, especially rural women and Indigenous women, it has also presented an opportunity for women to rise up in resistance, collective action, and coalition building for environmental justice and climate justice and take back the narrative! Women worldwide are working to create solutions to the pressing injustices magnified by the climate crisis. Let us learn more about some of these powerful activists, leaders, and organizers below. You can even incorporate these into your classroom by having students do research and create biographies or reports:

- *Lola Cabnal (Guatemala)*: A Mayan Q'eqchí woman from a rural community in the municipality of Livingston, Guatemala. One of the Indigenous peoples and civil society representatives to the UN-REDD Programme's Executive Board, where she has worked to elevate the perspective of Indigenous women and communities. Learn more here: https://www.un-redd.org/
- *Verónica Inmunda (Ecuador)*: A Kichwa woman from the Ecuadoran Amazon, she is the Youth, Culture and Sports Coordinator at CONFENIAE (Confederación de Nacionalidades Indígenas de la Amazonía Ecuatoriana). A law student studying the protection of Indigenous peoples' rights and is an advocate for integrating Indigenous knowledge and practices. Learn more here: https://confeniae.net/
- *Hindou Oumarou Ibrahim (Chad)*: A Mbororo Indigenous pastoralist woman, Hindou is the founder of the Association of Indigenous Peul Women and Peoples of Chad (AFPAT), a community-based organization that promotes environmental protection and the rights of women and girls in the Mbororo community. She is also an influential African climate leader who has championed traditional ecological knowledge as a means to cope with the climate crisis. Learn more here: http://www.afpat.net/
- *Grace Balawag (The Philippines)*: A Kankaney-Igorot Indigenous woman from the Philippines, she is the deputy coordinator for the Climate Change Adaptation and Mitigation Program of the Tebtebba-Indigenous Peoples' International Centre for Policy Research and Education. Learn more here: https://www.tebtebba.org/

What other ideas do you have for integrating some of these powerful change-makers into your classroom? Next, we will learn how Gen-Z is exploring various social movements for their activism and recognize the importance of centering intersectionality. Gen-Z artists are also using music as a platform for environmental and climate justice activism. Let's see the next section.

Gen-Z Activism Today

Centering Intersectionality

Leah Thomas is one of the most well-known Gen Z environmental activists and social media influencers. A self-described "eco-communicator," Thomas garnered much attention in 2020 during the national uprisings after the murder of George Floyd. A Black American, Thomas, and many others were dismayed and outraged by the environmental movement's silence during this time. In 2020, she posted her protest art to Instagram as a graphic that read, "Environmentalists for Black Lives Matter," and created another slide with her definition of "intersectional environmentalism" (Thomas, 2022). Suddenly, this post went viral, and she garnered national attention. Following this, she and other Gen-Z activists established the first Intersectional Environmentalist Council, comprising notable BIPOC activists, advocates, and influencers. They then built a database and resource hub with resources to disseminate to the general public.

However, you may be thinking that this concept sounds kind of familiar. This new Gen-Z activism has not been immune to critique, as it can be perceived as a "rebranded" version of environmental justice or environmental justice with a Gen-Z style. Dr. Robert Bullard, whom we learned about in earlier chapters, said,

> *I am not mad at anybody for coining a new term, but that is it. It is a term... It does not signify anything different than what we have already developed and institutionalized in the work. It is a catchy concept. It's trendy, it's sexy. However, how does it apply on the ground in communities that are fighting environmental racism?*
>
> (Oglesby, 2021)

Note that environmental justice, as a movement and a concept, was founded to counter environmental racism, so race and class were the original analytical factors. Moreover, what is missing from this new Gen-Z activism and Intersectional Environmentalism is an emphasis on intergenerational collaboration and learning with/from others. These are some key principles and elements of teaching environmental justice to K-5 students. Gen-Z's digital savvy and emphasis on social media and technology can indeed be useful tools in the fight for environmental justice. This new language and approach also resonates with young people today, making it valuable for recruiting more young people and students to advocate for environmental and climate justice. However, involving environmental professionals, environmental activists, and elders in the process is important because their wisdom and professional experience are invaluable. Recognizing, honoring, valuing, and appreciating those who have come before you is also imperative.

The Head and Heart Connection: Making Environmental Justice Protest Music

Let us learn more about Principle 2: Not Just a Science Issue. Movements for social change have a long history of using music to help elevate their causes!

Before social media and news channels existed, important information was often conveyed through songs. Harriet Tubman used spirituals to convey coded messages while she served as a conductor on the Underground Railroad. A song can also help elevate the truth or challenge the status quo in the American consciousness. For example, Tracy Chapman's song "Talkin' Bout a Revolution" in 1988 was fighting for the rights of the working class and poor and warned the rich that the status quo would be changed. Activist protest songs can inspire both your head and your heart. As you may recall from an earlier chapter, J. Drew Lanham discussed this head-and-heart connection, which manifests in his unique blend of the arts, activism, and science.

Time to explore some environmental justice protest songs that challenge "green business as usual" and "the green status quo." You can use these songs in your classroom to inspire students. Your students can study the musical artist who wrote/sang/performed the song, they can remix or rewrite the lyrics, perform their own versions of the song, analyze the lyrics for social movement meaning and context, make stop-motion or claymation videos of the song, or film and act out their own music videos! Many possibilities would impact a wide range of content areas and various standards (Table 4.6). There are also many possibilities for captivating student interest and tapping into "kid culture."

Now What? How This Book Can Help

You have now finished Part II: The First Steps—Shifting the Focus From Mainstream Environmentalism to Environmental Justice. Congratulations! We have continued to learn about the Principles and Elements of Environmental Justice for K-5 students and what this can look like in the classroom. I hope that the fifth-grade National Park truth detectives in Chapter 3 and this chapter's fourth-grade natural disaster analysts have both helped you to see these principles and elements alive and in action, particularly Principle 1: Encourage Student Questions and Observations, with an emphasis on Element 2: Aim to Cultivate and Develop a Critical Consciousness. This principle and the corresponding element are crucial in equipping our students. It provides them with the tools to disrupt the "green status quo" and "green business as usual," as we aim to shift instruction to center on justice and equity. In addition, we have continued to learn about Principle 3: In Community with Elders, Activists, and Environmental Professionals. Intergenerational collaboration across disciplines is essential in the work to promote environmental justice. We have also further examined the Learning for Justice Social Justice Standards and a concept called "intersectionality," both of which can help center lived environmental experiences of all students and teach for environmental

Table 4.6 Environmental Protest Songs

Musical Artist	Song Name	Song Theme	Available Resources
Common, Malik Yusef, Mumasi Featuring Aaron Fresh, Choklate, Laci Kay	Trouble in the Water	Environmental justice; Environmental Racism; Flint Water Crisis	Link to Music Video: https://youtu.be/qDUY3eXv-UY?feature=shared
Billie Eilish	All The Good Girls Go To Hell	Climate Change; Oil Spills	Billie Eilish Talking about the Environmental Inspiration for the Video: https://youtu.be/KZYDUw37Js0?feature=shared
Billie Eilish	Ocean Eyes	Climate Change, Pollution, and Climate Justice	Link to Music Video: https://youtu.be/viimfQi_pUw?feature=shared
Halluci Nation, featuring DJ and producer Boogey the Beat & Northern Voice	Land Back	Decolonization; Land Back Movement	Official music video: https://youtu.be/67F7WbcTQKA?feature=shared Note: The Halluci Nation would like to dedicate this song in support of the Wet'suwet'en Nation and to the Indigenous movements across Turtle Island and beyond.
Taboo and Magnificent Seven	Stand Up/ Stand N Rock #NoDAPL **Winner of an MTV VMA for Best Fight Against the System	Land Back; Decolonization; Dakota Access Pipeline Protests	Link to Music Video: https://youtu.be/Onyk7guvHK8?feature=shared
Raye Zaragoza	In the River	Land Back; Decolonization; Dakota Access Pipeline Protests	Link to Music Video: https://youtu.be/l4eosRdP5gQ?feature=shared

(Continued)

Table 4.6 (Continued)

Musical Artist	Song Name	Song Theme	Available Resources
Ta'Kaiya Blaney	Earth Revolution	Climate Emergency, Indigenous Rights, Climate Justice	Link to Music Video: https://youtu.be/l9tTdy4OnQs?feature=shared
Bonnie Raitt, Indigo Girls, Mumu Fresh, Winona LaDuke, and More	No More Pipeline Blues	Decolonization, Land Back, Dakota Access Pipeline Protests	Link to Music Video: https://youtu.be/zjoRB7ETaGk?feature=shared

justice and climate justice. To reflect on what you learned in this first section, consider the following reflection questions about your professional practice. Before moving on, do not forget to check out the Further Reading section for resources for students and teachers from this chapter!

Reflections Questions for Professional Practice

Chapter 4 Questions

- What are some other pop-culture connections that you can make to hook students for lessons?
- What are some other ways that you can think of to integrate music and musical artists into your environmental justice lessons?
- How might you incorporate Indigenous women climate activists into your curriculum?
- How does learning about the concept of intersectionality further your understanding of teaching environmental justice? Or the need to introduce environmental justice?

Further Reading: Resources for Teachers and Students

Videos and Resources for Teachers

Action for the Climate Emergency. *Hurricane Maria in Puerto Rico: Youth & Climate.* Youtube. https://www.youtube.com/watch?v=fy-wG8AVsao&utm_medium=ref&utm_source=ref_ocof&utm_campaign=educ

Democracy Now. *We cannot wait: Puerto Rico's residents organize to provide food & water after Hurricane Maria.* https://www.democracynow.org/2017/10/2/voices_from_san_juan_puerto_rico

Flores, G. (2024). *Bad Bunny Unleashes Poignant 'Una Velita,' Reflecting on Puerto Rico's Political Climate.* Billboard. https://www.billboard.com/music/latin/bad-bunny-una-velita-puerto-rico-political-climate-hurricane-maria-1235780425/

Learning for Justice. *Intersectionality 101.* Youtube. https://www.youtube.com/watch?v=w6dnj2IyYjE

MacArthur Foundation. *Catherine Coleman Flowers, Environmental Health Advocate, 2020 MacArthur Foundation Fellow.* YouTube. https://youtu.be/aID_EdPUMNg?feature=shared

Mr. Alicia's Arcade of Knowledge. *Alicia and the hurricane: A story of Puerto Rico read aloud.* Youtube. https://youtu.be/pNjOjzWOpeQ?feature=shared

SubjectToClimate. *Women and climate change guide.* https://subjecttoclimate.org/teacher-guides/women-and-climate-change-guide

TED. *Climate justice cannot happen without racial justice: David Lammy.* https://www.youtube.com/watch?v=EkIpeO1r0NI

TED. *How to build an equitable and just climate future: Peggy Shepard.* https://www.youtube.com/watch?v=j-rw3x8VZxA

Books for Teachers

Ahn, E. (2024). *Advocate: A graphic memoir of family, community, and the fight for environmental justice.* Emeryville, CA: Ten Speed Graphic.

Flowers, C. C. (2022). *Waste: One woman's fight against America's dirty secret.* New York, NY: The New Press.

Flowers, C. C. (2025). *Holy ground: On activism, environmental justice, and finding hope.* New York, NY: Spiegel & Grau.

Kormos, A. (2024). *Intertwined: Women, nature, and climate justice.* New York, NY: The New Press.

Lim, A. (2021). *The world we need: Stories and lessons from America's unsung environmental movement.* New York, NY: New Press.

Lloréns, H. (2021). *Making livable worlds: Afro-Puerto Rican women building environmental justice.* Seattle, WA: University of Washington Press.

Sigwalt, D. (2022). *This book will save the planet: A climate-justice primer for activists and changemakers.* London: Frances Lincoln Children's Books.

Thomas, L. (2022). *The intersectional environmentalist: How to dismantle systems of oppression to protect people and the planet.* New York, NY: Voracious.

Warner, A. (2023). *Rise up and sing! Power, protest, and activism in music.* Vancouver: Greystone Kids.

Picture Books for Students

Bogan, C. (2017). *Where is Rodney?* San Francisco, CA: Yosemite Conservancy.

Harrington, J. (2019). *Buzzing with questions: The inquisitive mind of Charles Henry Turner.* New York. NY. Calkins Creek.

Mangal, M. (2021). *Jayden's impossible garden.* Minneapolis, MN: Free Spirit Publishing.

Newman, L. (2022). *Alicia and the hurricane/Alicia Y El Huracán: A story of Puerto Rico/Un cuento de Puerto Rico.* San Francisco, CA: Children's Book Press (CBP).

Robertson, J. (2017). *Water walker.* Toronto: Second Story Press.

Watson, R. (2014). *A place where hurricanes happen.* Decorah, IA: Dragonfly Books.

References

Catherine Coleman Flowers. (n.d). https://www.catherinecolemanflowers.com/

Chapola, J., Datta, R., Waucaush-Warn, J., & Subroto, S. (2024). Climate change and its impact on the mental health and well-being of Indigenous women in Western cities, Canada. *Journal of Community & Applied Social Psychology, 34*(3), e2807.

Flowers, C. C. (2020). *Waste: One woman's fight against America's dirty secret.* New York, NY: The New Press.

Food and Agriculture Organization of the United States (FAO). (2024). *The unjust climate – Measuring the impacts of climate change on rural poor, women and youth.* Rome. https://doi.org/10.4060/cc9680en

McCarthy, J. (2020). Understanding why climate change impacts women more than men. *Global Citizen.* https://www.globalcitizen.org/en/content/how-climate-change-affects-women/

Moulton, H. (2024). Indigenous women are the "guardians of Pachamama." Territorial sovereignty is indispensable for just climate change adaptations in Peru. *Global Environmental Change, 89,* 102934.

Moulton, H., & Carey, M. (2023). Future making in a disaster zone: Everyday climate change adaptation amongst Quechua women in the Peruvian Cordillera Blanca. *Environmental Science & Policy, 148,* 103551.

Oglesby, C. (2021, Feb 10). *The generational rift over 'intersectional environmentalism': Environmental justice got a Gen Z makeover.* Grist. https://grist.org/justice/intersectional-environmentalism-justice-language/

Stone, L., & McClellan. M. (2024, January 22). *Catherine Coleman Flowers: A disruptor in the best sense.* RMI. https://rmi.org/catherine-coleman-flowers-a-disruptor-in-the-best-sense/

Thomas, L. (2022). *The intersectional environmentalist: How to dismantle systems of oppression to protect people and the planet.* New York, NY: Voracious.

Winkler, I. T., & Flowers, C. C. (2017). America's dirty secret: The human right to sanitation in Alabama's Black Belt. *Columbia Human Rights Law Review, 49*, 181.

Part 3

Implementing the First Steps—A Toolkit of Curricular Entry Points

Part 3 provides some easy entry points in a "plug and play" style toolkit that teachers can implement into their existing curriculum. There are connections across the curriculum, which include but are not limited to: Next Generation Science Standards (NGSS), Common Core State Standards, the College, Career, and Civic Life (C3) Framework, the National Council for the Social Studies Curricular Themes, National Geography Standards, and more. In Chapter 5, we will continue learning about Principle 2: Not Just a Science Issue, and Element 1: Engagement and Entry Points Across the Curriculum. In addition, we will continue to examine Principle 3: In Community with Elders, Activists, and Environmental Professionals, and Element 2: Learning with/from Others. In this chapter's spotlight, learn from a first-grade class studying the importance of art in the fight for intersectional environmental justice.

5

A Toolkit of Initial Starting Points for Teaching Environmental Justice

Spotlight: First-Grade Environmental Justice Artists

"Class, Class," said Ms. Thompson. "Yes, yes!" responded the energetic first graders, recognizing the class call for attention. Once she had all eyes on her, Ms. Thompson continued.

"Today, for our art lesson, we will learn about a famous artist named Favianna Rodriguez. Artists can use their work to teach the public about larger issues like social justice and environmental justice," said Ms. Thompson.

Now let us review our vocabulary word: Intersectionality. Remember, that is a college word.

"We can go to college!" said Lupe proudly. "Exactly," said Mrs. Thompson.

Great, my scholars. Can someone remind me what this word means?
Ms. Thompson, it was like a puzzle. Like each person, like a puzzle, we all get different puzzle pieces…like what language you speak, or where your family is from. Alternatively, whether you are rich or not. Alternatively, if you go to church or whatnot…

said Dwyane.

"Excellent, Dwyane, that is correct. Intersectionality is like the combination of the different puzzle pieces that make up the whole person. We made those puzzle posters of ourselves and our own intersectional identities, right class?"

DOI: 10.4324/9781003620709-9

"Yeah, Ms. Thompson, they are over there!" several voices shouted as they excitedly pointed towards the back wall.

"Excellent, that is right!" said Ms. Thompson. "Today, we are going to do another art project, and we are going to do it in the style of Favianna Rodriguez. We are going to make climate justice art posters. I know how much you all love art!"

"Our guiding question is: How do artists like Favianna Rodriguez use art to address environmental justice and climate justice?" Ms. Thompson approached the board and wrote the question for students to see. Next to the question were the learning objectives:

- Describe how artists can bring about change through artmaking.
- Explain how art can be used to address climate change.
- Express a personal response to an artist's work about climate change.

"First, learn about Favianna and look at some of her artwork. Felix, can you get the lights, please?" said Ms. Thompson as she turned on the projector and pulled down the screen.

"Okay, so here is some of Favianna's artwork (slide deck here: https://s3.amazonaws.com/favianna-staging/resources/files/f962ce310bae42d7abc9061d95c44437.pdf). As we can see from her work, she cares about our college word, intersectionality, which appears in many of her works. Let's explore the climate justice art gallery."

"I will give each of your table groups two printouts of her art from the slideshow. Now, I want you to discuss these two questions in your table group: (1) What do you notice about her art? (2) How does it make you feel? You can write some ideas in your notebooks, and then I will call representatives for answers. I will give it seven minutes."

After the timer went off, Mrs. Thompson said, "Okay, I heard some great ideas. I would love to hear what you all came up with."

"Ms. Thomson, we see many colors in her work," said Lisa. "She also uses many lines…straight, curved, zig-zag. "The lines are always thick and black, like how we outline things in a Sharpie!" said Yousef.

"Her work excites me." Like the picture is moving and it has energy" said Marco.

"Excellent work, artists," said Ms. Thompson. "We are going to be inspired by her style of art, so that means using warm, bold colors, and thick black lines. Furthermore, making sure our images have much movement to them."

Let us watch this video, and now she will show us how to make a social and environmental justice poster like her: https://www.youtube.com/watch?v=-88O4ISw8Gk

> *Next, after watching her instructions in the video, here are some of the shapes that she has given us to use, which are on her website: https://s3.amazonaws.com/favianna-staging/resources/files/b0ce8a1e42f94bb49a52c66194cbfdb6.pdf*
>
> *Table captains, please go get the art buckets from the back table. The buckets contain enough materials for the table: construction paper, copies of her shapes, markers, crayons, pencils, glue, and erasers. Please make sure to save paper scraps for our recycling bin; we will use them for another art project.*
>
> *"I cannot wait to see what all of you great artists come up with," said Ms. Thompson. "When we are done making our posters, we should ask Principal Garcia if we can hang them in the library or the cafeteria so other people can enjoy them and also learn about Favianna Rodriguez's work."*

After learning from the first-grade environmental justice artists, it is time to unpack some of the key takeaways from this lesson! To address Element 2: Aim to Cultivate and Develop a Critical Consciousness, Ms. Thompson reviewed the "college word" of intersectionality. To make intersectionality relevant and digestible for first-graders, the class learned about a puzzle as a metaphor. As an art extension, the students created self-portraits using puzzle pieces to begin grappling with this concept. Older students in upper elementary grades might begin to grapple with understanding how power and privilege intersect, and the teacher can use a personal identity wheel if students are learning the vocabulary. There is a handout with a wheel that upper-elementary students can understand. This is linked in the resources section at the end of this chapter.

In the lesson, Ms. Thompson utilized the excellent educational resources available on Favianna Rodriguez's website. Ms. Thompson also posed the guiding question, How do artists like Favianna Rodriguez use art to address environmental and climate justice issues? The learning objectives on the board were: (1) Describe how artists can impact change through artmaking; (2) Explain ways that art can be used to address climate change; (3) Express a personal response to an artist's work about climate change. These learning objectives also fulfill Principle 2: Not Just a Science Issue, and Element 1: Engagement and Entry Points across the Curriculum. In addition, this lesson also addresses Principle 3: In Community with Elders, Activists, and Environmental Professionals, and Element 2: Learning with/from Others. The first-grade artists were also excited to ask the principal if they could display their posters in the cafeteria or the school library! This is an excellent opportunity for students to learn about art exhibitions and how they can create their own galleries or exhibitions, just like real artists and activists. This spotlight from the first-graders brings us to the first starting point in our toolkit: Creating an intersectional environmental justice art exhibition or an art build. There are ideas and resources that you can implement immediately in your classroom. Time to take a look!

Starting Points and Initial Ideas to Pair with Existing Curriculum

Starting Point 1: Intersectional Environmental Justice and the Arts

Arts integration is a powerful tool in teaching environmental justice! Experts have found that arts integration not only enhances students' learning experiences by encouraging creativity, emotional expression, and critical thinking, but it can also enhance students' overall cognitive development (Clements, 2024). According to the National Art Education Association, arts integration fosters a more profound understanding across various disciplines and provides students with authentic and engaging learning experiences. To make arts integration effective, it should also aim to address the National Core Arts Standards and standards from other curricular content areas (National Core Arts Standards, 2015). The National Core Arts Standards are aligned with four artistic processes: Creating, Presenting, Responding, and Connecting. All these processes will help foster artistic literacy and competency in students. Within each artistic process, there are corresponding anchor standards. In addition, there are standards for the visual arts, dance, music, theater, and media arts. Effective arts integration can also help students make connections between themselves, others, and the world, which is key for teaching and learning about environmental justice. Look at a streamlined version of the National Visual Arts Standards in Table 5.1, and some ideas you can implement in your classroom!

Visual Arts Artistic Process of Creating: Curate an Environmental Justice Art Exhibition
- **Choose a Location:** In addition to displaying the art in various locations throughout the school, another idea might be to partner with a local coffee shop that's willing to host a "gallery" or "exhibition" of student work. Additionally, consider visiting your local city library or a youth center.
- **Create an Event:** Students can help organize an "environmental justice art night" at school. The school PTA might be willing to help, along with parent volunteers or local environmental justice organizations! If your school or district has an after-school arts program, an art specialist, or an art teacher, enlist their help! Students can even have a fundraiser or art showcase and donate the proceeds to an environmental justice organization in their local community or state.

Table 5.1 National Visual Arts Standards

Visual Arts Artistic Process	Anchor Standard	Ideas for the Classroom
Creating	• Anchor Standard 1: Generate and conceptualize artistic ideas and work • Anchor Standard 2: Organize and develop artistic ideas and work • Anchor Standard 3: Refine and complete artistic work	• Like professional artists, students can curate an intersectional environmental justice art exhibition! This has excellent potential for wider parent and community involvement. Learn more in the following section.
Presenting	• Anchor Standard 4: Select, analyze, and interpret artistic work for presentation • Anchor Standard 5: Develop and refine artistic techniques and work for presentation • Anchor Standard 6: Convey meaning through the presentation of artistic work	• You can help your students host an intersectional environmental justice art build to develop their competency as artist-activists and community organizers. • An intersectional environmental justice art build is a great way to culminate a unit on environmental justice and create entry points for wider parent and community involvement. This will also help students learn about the work of artist-activists and the role of art in movement-building for environmental justice. Learn more in the following section.
Responding	• Anchor Standard 7: Perceive and analyze artistic work • Anchor Standard 8: Interpret intent and meaning in artistic work • Anchor Standard 9: Apply criteria to evaluate artistic work	• Spotlight activity: Favianna Rodriguez's work. • Have students respond to the work of these artist-activists who work at the intersections of art and environmental justice. All of these artists have websites with examples of their work: a Ricardo Levins Morales b Davis Solnit c Jill Pelto

(Continued)

Table 5.1 (*Continued*)

Visual Arts Artistic Process	Anchor Standard	Ideas for the Classroom
Connecting	• Anchor Standard 10: Synthesize and relate knowledge and personal experiences to make art • Anchor Standard 11: Relate artistic ideas and works with societal, cultural, and historical context to deepen understanding	• Connect to other social studies, math, science, art disciplines, or literacy content standards. • Hip-Hop and Place-Based Environmental Justice Pedagogy is an excellent way for students to incorporate music and popular culture. Learn more in the section below.

- **Grade-Level Curator or Class Curator:** Different grades or classes can have different themes and curate a gallery with corresponding themes or topics. These "galleries" can be in different locations in the school.
- **Write a Student Artist Statement:** An artist statement should be two to three sentences in length, explaining how the work relates to the art exhibition themes. Students can write about why their work is important to them, details about their artistic process, or anything else notable about their work.
- **Artwork Labels:** Each artwork should have labels that include the artist's name, the title of the work, and the medium used to create it. The artist's statement should also appear on the label.
- **Content Connections:** Students can also write reflections or essays to accompany their artist statements, thereby fulfilling writing standards. Consider compiling the writing into an exhibition catalogue. At an exhibition or gallery night, students can also practice speaking and listening skills by presenting their work to visitors and giving a presentation. Students can also apply math by calculating measurements for layout and gallery installation, or by counting money earned from a fundraiser.

Visual Arts Artistic Process of Presenting: Host an Intersectional Environmental Justice Art Build

Students can learn about "art builds" by studying the work of David Solnit, listed above. Artists Favianna Rodriguez and Ricardo Levins Morales are also very active in utilizing their work during art builds and movements for social and environmental justice. An art build often precedes a movement or an action for racial justice or climate justice, such as a protest. An art build is a great way to mobilize a group of people around an event or cause, bring together volunteers, and foster a sense of community. Here are some steps to host an art build below:

- **Find a Location:** The school gymnasium, cafeteria, or local park. A flat surface is essential, especially when the group is creating posters. There should also be ample room for supplies like paints and buckets.
- **Structure of Art Build:** Will people choose to work on their projects, such as posters, or join a larger group project, like painting large banners? Will you just provide the materials, and people do as they please? Or does the build have a clear goal and a specific visual goal output?
- **Volunteers:** This is a good opportunity to invite parent volunteers, the PTA, the school community, local organizations, or local artists. What will the volunteers do? Will they help clean up? Help set up? Consider offering time slots and specific shifts that volunteers can choose from. If you are hosting a more casual type of art build, volunteers can also drop in at their convenience.
- **Materials:** Consider gathering recycled materials ahead of time that can be used and saved for art projects. For example (1) Cardboard; (2) Fabrics; (3) Bed Sheets; (4) Sticks and Poles; (5) Scrap Paper; (6) Butcher Paper; (7) Paint; (8) Markers; (9) Dried markers that can be put in water and used as watercolors; (10) A clothesline and pins to hang wet posters on. Also, consider asking the PTA for donations. Go to local grocery stores and ask for cardboard boxes. The dollar store is another good option for cheap materials.
- **Invite the Media:** Consider inviting the local news to the event. Your school or district might also have a district communications person to help spread the news. Make sure to play music during the event, and have fun!

Now that you are equipped with some starting points for teaching your students about how artists like Favianna Rodriguez and others use art as a catalyst to address environmental justice and climate justice, your students or school can host their own intersectional environmental justice art exhibition or an intersectional environmental justice art build. To continue with Principle 2: Not Just a Science Issue, and Element 1: Engagement and Entry Points across the Curriculum, let us look at music and environmental justice!

Visual Arts Artistic Process of Connecting: Hip-Hop and Place-Based Environmental Justice Pedagogy

In Chapter 4, we learned from the fourth-grade natural disaster analysts, who were making connections between music and activism. They learned that musicians can use their platform to elevate larger issues of social justice and even environmental justice, and can help engage the public in the three elements/components of critical consciousness. We also learned that activist protest songs can inspire both head and heart. This head-and-heart connection is something that J. Drew Lanham believes in and nurtures in his work, where he blends ecology, writing, and social justice. We also previously learned about environmental justice protest songs in Chapter 4 that challenge "green business as usual" and "the green status quo." Let us keep learning more.

Hip-hop has long been a means for artists to convey their critical consciousness by analyzing their immediate surroundings, critiquing injustices in the built environment, and highlighting the struggles and daily life in communities. Hip-hop is also a way to highlight the role and function of urban ecology, place-based learning, and music education. Hip-hop can serve as a means to foster critical consciousness, providing a valuable entry point for teaching about environmental racism. Next, learn about another environmental professional who uses hip-hop to disrupt the "green status quo" and "green business as usual."

DJ Caveem (https://www.chefietef.com/) is a vegan chef, rapper, and nutritional educator. Growing up in an urban city with limited healthy food options, he developed community-based initiatives that teach about urban gardening and plant-based nutrition, complemented by cooking, gardening, and music courses for children. These themes, including food justice, environmental justice, and nutrition, also appear in his musical lyrics. He continues this message in his advertising and outreach. For example, his album *Biomimicz* was released with a recipe for vegan dishes and a seed pack! The link is here to explore: https://djcavem.bandcamp.com/album/biomimicz. DJ Caveem can provide students with a real-life example of an environmental professional who also uses music to raise awareness about environmental justice issues. Other topics that appear in DJ Caveem's music are the availability and access to organic food in urban communities of color and environmental racism.

For example, DJ Caveem's 2021 song "Pull Up on the Gate" offers commentary on environmental racism. In the video, he pulls up in a landscape truck to an affluent White neighborhood, which provides an analysis of how people of color are viewed as the landscapers taking care of the gardens of the elite while simultaneously experiencing a lack of greenery in their neighborhoods due to urban density and redlining. Students can watch the video here: https://youtu.be/ETr8z03Typc?feature=shared. As a starting point, students can explore issues of tree equity in their neighborhoods and surrounding areas by visiting the Tree Equity website: https://www.treeequityscore.org/. Students can use the national map to find the "tree equity score," uncover the hidden story of where trees are in the community, and then make the case with data and reports by comparing tree equity scores among neighborhoods. Students can even compose their own lyrics or music videos about tree equity or tree inequity in their neighborhoods and communities: Exciting! Now that we have examined some starting points for intersectional environmental justice and art, we will move on to explore some initial approaches to environmental justice and literacy.

Starting Point 2: Environmental Justice and Literacy

Be sure to refer to the resources section at the end of each chapter for recommended picture books to use in your classroom. Picture books are an excellent way to introduce students to the concepts of natural disasters and environmental racism. They serve as an entry point to lessons that can help increase their critical literacy and foster the development of their critical consciousness. First, time to examine Hurricane Katrina and how it can catalyze learning about not only environmental racism but also community resilience. After we unpack teaching about Hurricane Katrina and natural disasters, take this further with some picture books and lesson plan ideas.

Unpacking Hurricane Katrina and Natural Disasters

Remember where you were when you learned about Hurricane Katrina? Hurricane Katrina was one of the most devastating, deadly, and costly natural disasters in United States history. In late August 2005, the north-central Gulf Coast was severely hit, destroying the coast of Mississippi, Alabama, and Louisiana, with the worst damage occurring in New Orleans. In New Orleans, nearly all of the levees were breached, flooding almost the entire city and several neighboring parishes. Approximately 1,800 people lost their lives. As educators committed to equity and justice, taking into consideration what we learned about environmental racism in previous chapters, we recognize that these tragedies were not experienced equally by everyone. Also, reflecting on what we learned in previous chapters about the history of the environmental justice movement, we know that the federal government is not always responsive, particularly when it comes to inequities that disproportionately affect communities of color.

Do your students know what a press conference is? According to the Congressional Black Caucus (n.d.), Hurricane Katrina illuminated the vulnerability of low-income communities and people of color to environmental disasters, as many New Orleans Black residents were stranded, displaced, and left permanently homeless by Katrina. Water, medicine, and food shortages were significant issues of this humanitarian crisis. Members of the Congressional Black Caucus (CBC) were very active and vocal in their advocacy for Hurricane Katrina victims. On September 2, 2005, a joint press conference was held to call attention to these injustices. Students can watch the press conference here: *Congressional Black Caucus Hurricane Katrina Press Conference on CSPAN*: https://www.c-span.org/search/?For=congressional%20black%20caucus%20katrina. As an extension of this advocacy strategy, students can create a press conference to draw attention to local environmental injustice issues in their communities. Consider inviting the school district's communications team, parents, community members, or local news outlets.

How do you think New Orleans residents view federal relief efforts? The Pew Research Center (2005) conducted a national poll a week after the storm, which found that Black New Orleanians were highly critical of the federal government's relief efforts. In the poll results, 66% of Black respondents believed, "the government's response to the situation would have been faster if most of the victims had been white." The Reverend Al Sharpton echoed these results and stated, "I feel that, if it were in another area, with another economic stratum and racial makeup, that President Bush would have run out of Crawford a lot quicker and FEMA would have found its way in a lot sooner" (Garaad, 2023, p.11). This is also something students can explore: Federal response times to natural disasters in different communities or countries. Students can also research Hurricane Maria in Puerto Rico and the 2010 earthquake in Haiti.

For more in-depth studies with your class, Ochoa-Becker (2006) provides five types of questions to inspire student thinking about the intersections of environmental justice, human rights, and natural disasters:

1   What does human rights mean? (Definitional Question)
2   When people are affected by a natural disaster, what human rights come into play? (Evidential Question)
3   When human rights are violated or violated after a disaster, what should the government do? (Policy Question)
4   Are there good reasons for people to avoid involvement in any human rights issue related to a natural disaster? (Value Question)
5   What position would you take if your city or town were designated as a resettlement area for disaster victims? (Speculative Question).

Remember Drs. Bullard and Wright? We learned about these leaders in the environmental justice movement in previous chapters. They held a similar belief that the impact of natural disasters is far from natural because they are rooted in the segregation of impoverished communities and racialized communities (Bullard & Wright, 2009). Here, we can see that environmental justice and civil rights are closely connected, representing two sides of the same coin. For curricular ideas to implement immediately in your classroom, refer to Table 5.2 for resources on teaching about extreme weather and natural disasters. There are various picture books and extension ideas that can be implemented across the curriculum.

Table 5.2 Teaching about Natural Disasters and Extreme Weather

Book	Natural Disaster	Curricular Ideas and Resources
"Marvelous Cornelius: Hurricane Katrina and the Spirit of New Orleans" by Phil Bildner	Hurricane Katrina	• The role/importance of sanitation workers in the Environmental Justice Movement • Art lesson ideas with reflection and discussion questions: https://seldallas.org/unit-12-skill-building-marvelous-cornelius/
"A Storm Called Katrina" by Myron Uhlberg	Hurricane Katrina	• Curricular resources from Teaching Books: https://school.teachingbooks.net/tb.cgi?tid=29374 • STEM and ELA lesson plan: https://wp.wpi.edu/iamstem/2023/086/grade-4-a-storm-called-katrina/
"The Coquíes Still Sing: A Story of Home, Hope, and Rebuilding" by Karina Nicole González	Hurricane Maria	• Start a community garden project in your local community • Learn about Coquíes and the Taino people: https://folkways.si.edu/el-coqui/music/tools-for-teaching/smithsonian • Other lesson plan ideas and discussion questions: https://www.learningtogive.org/resources/coquies-still-sing
"Hope for Haiti" by Jesse Joshua Watson	Haiti Earthquake	• Resources for teaching about the Earthquake in Haiti: http://briefings.dadeschools.net/files/100148_haiti_earthquake_instructional_resources.pdf • The Aid Dilemma: https://www.pbs.org/wgbh/pages/frontline/teach/haitiaid/lesson.html (Can be modified for upper elementary students)

Starting Point 3: Integrating Youth Activists into Your Curriculum

Throughout the book, numerous profiles of youth activists are provided, which you can incorporate into your curriculum, along with ideas for integrating youth voices. Now, time to dive deeper and examine a social studies unit plan that teaches about youth activists and environmental advocacy. One reason social studies complements environmental justice lessons is that it provides the ideal foundation for taking informed action and pursuing civic engagement.

Are you familiar with the C3 Framework? The College, Career, and Civic Life Framework (C3 Framework) from the National Council for the Social Studies (2013) enhances the rigor of the disciplines of social studies; builds critical thinking, problem-solving, and participatory skills for engaged citizens; and aligns with the Common Core State Standards for English Language Arts and Literacy in History/Social Studies. The Inquiry Arc of the C3 Framework was designed with four dimensions of informed inquiry in social studies: (1) developing questions and planning inquiries; (2) applying disciplinary concepts and tools; (3) evaluating sources and using evidence; and (4) communicating conclusions and taking informed action. Dimension 4 of the College, Career, and Civic Life Framework is taking informed action—time to explore some indicators of dimension 4 below (Table 5.3).

Compelling Question: What actions can students take to protect the environment?

Table 5.3 Taking Informed Action for Environmental Justice

By the End of Grade 2	By the End of Grade 5
D4.6.K-2. Identify and explain a range of local, regional, and global problems and some ways in which people are trying to address these problems	**D4.6.3–5.** Draw on disciplinary concepts to explain the challenges people have faced and opportunities they have created in addressing local, regional, and global problems at various times and places.
D4.7.K-2. Identify ways to take action to help address local, regional, and global problems	**D4.7.3–5.** Explain different strategies and approaches students and others could take in working alone and together to address local, regional, and global problems, and predict possible results of their actions.
D4.8.K-2. Use listening, consensus-building, and voting procedures to decide on and act in their classrooms.	**D4.8.3–5.** Use a range of deliberative and democratic procedures to make decisions about and act on civic problems in their classrooms and schools.

Individually and with Others, Students…

See how this leads to a compelling question. Students can examine and analyze primary source photos of youth activists at a climate protest. Use some historical photos from the events of the history of the Environmental Justice Movement in Chapter 1, and a specific protest or direct action in your local community. Use these sentence starters to help guide students' explorations of the photos: I see _____, I think_____, I wonder _____, I predict_____. Giant Post-its or butcher paper would work great for a gallery walk around the room. Students can record their thoughts at each station. Another idea would be for students to collaborate with peers or in small groups on a Google Slides deck.

Next, students can learn about real-life examples of youth activists taking action for environmental and climate justice. Table 5.4 contains a graphic organizer that you can use in your classroom. After watching the case-study videos of youth activists, students can analyze how youth are engaging in advocacy, action, and mobilization by answering the remaining questions in the graphic organizer. This is an excellent opportunity for students to practice their research skills and conduct interviews with students in their community.

Table 5.4 Youth Activism Graphic Organizer

Video Example of Youth Activism	Teen Fights for Toxic Waste Cleanup (PBS): https://thinktv.pbslearningmedia.org/resource/envh10.sci.life.eco.superfund/teen-fights-for-toxic-waste-cleanup/	Teen Maps Contaminants from Coal Plant (PBS): https://thinktv.pbslearningmedia.org/resource/envh10.health.coalmap/teen-maps-contaminants-from-a-coal-plant/	Pacific Climate Warriors Rally: https://www.youtube.com/watch?v=CjFA0PYeeK0&t=2s
Environmental Conditions Being Objected to			
Government Reaction			
Youth/Student's Actions			
Challenges Faced			

This activity and exercise present an opportunity for students to learn about Superfunds. A "Superfund" refers to the Comprehensive Environmental Response, Compensation, and Liability Act (CERCLA), which is a federal law that aims to address the cleanup of hazardous waste sites. A "trust fund" is provided to address uncontrolled or abandoned sites. Students can learn more here on the EPA website: https://www.epa.gov/superfund. Students can explore the Superfund Site Search page from the EPA (https://www.epa.gov/superfund) to research Superfund sites in their state, community, or town. Students can answer the following questions:

- Location
- Name of the Superfund site
- Why is this Superfund a problem? What are the environmental or health impacts?
- What, if anything, has been done so far? Have the citizens or the government taken any actions?
- What actions need to continue?
- References list

To further extend their learning, students can start compiling their research into a report or presentation and contact their state's EPA, city council, representative, or principal. Students can also create social media campaigns and contact local environmental justice organizations in the area to partner with them for a protest or direct action.

An essential part of environmental justice education for elementary students is helping them learn about individuals who have bravely confronted the environmental crisis, including current youth activists, elders, and environmental professionals. Let us continue learning with Principle 3: In Community with Elders, Activists, and Environmental Professionals, and Element 2: Learning with/from Others. Next up is starting point 4, which will help students learn how the foundational documents from the Environmental Justice Movement are utilized today.

Starting Point 4: Information Texts and Primary Source Documents

The 17 Principles of Environmental Justice

One of the fantastic aspects of the 17 Principles of Environmental Justice is that it was written by real frontline community members who are the most directly impacted by environmental harms. On October 24, 1991, 300 minority activists gathered in Washington, DC, at the historic National People of Color

Environmental Leadership Summit to discuss the environmental injustices affecting their communities. In four days, they drafted the 17 Principles of Environmental Justice, which is considered a defining document of the Environmental Justice Movement. Many original documents from the First National People of Color Environmental Leadership Summit are still available and function as primary source documents that students can explore and analyze. Here are some ideas to get started:

- **Watch a Documentary on the Summit:** Students can examine the participants' speeches and how they worked on writing the principles: https://youtu.be/fo9uaWbhpPc?feature=shared
- **Read the Summit's Proceedings:** https://rescarta.ucc.org/jsp/RcWebImageViewer.jsp?doc_id=32092eb9-294e-4f6e-a880-17b8bbe02d88/OhClUCC0/00000001/00000070&pg_seq=1&search_doc=
- **30th Anniversary Celebration:** Students can look at photographs and interviews about the Summit on the United Church of Christ's website. https://www.ucc.org/30th-anniversary-the-first-national-people-of-color-environmental-leadership-summit/
- **Read the 17 Principles of Environmental Justice:** The original document is linked here http://lvejo.org/wp-content/uploads/2015/04/ej-jemez-principles.pdf

Students can also examine the 17 Principles of Environmental Justice and write a localized version for their school or local community. This is a great collaborative activity to recruit other classes or even your entire grade level! Once students have written their own 17 Principles of Environmental Justice, they may represent these ideas on posters, infographics, banners, or a pledge hanging in the classroom. Students might even check if their city or town has a Sustainability Office and if their city government has established any principles that they can learn about, adapt, or enhance. To practice digital literacy skills, students can make an interactive flipbook of their principles and publish it using a platform like Book Creator or Issuu, which will help share their findings with the broader community.

As an alternative idea, older students can examine other primary source documents, such as the Declaration of Independence, and compare and contrast them with the 17 Principles of Environmental Justice. Students can also share their findings with the class or with a buddy in a grade-level class. So far in this book, we have examined environmental justice from a U.S.-based perspective. Next, consider how environmental justice plays out internationally to add global connections and corresponding entry points.

Starting Point 5: Global and Intersectional Environmental Justice Movements

Remember Dr. Robert Bullard? While his work is U.S.-based mainly, he believes that disrupting the "green status quo" and "green business as usual" is a global effort. For example, restoring communities to their pre-damaged state after the harm caused by the fossil fuel industry is a key focus of the Environmental Justice Movement. He explains that global reparations are translated into the Loss and Damage Fund, a pot of money made by wealthier countries at the 2022 United Nations Climate Change Conference. This historic agreement was established to assist vulnerable nations in mitigating the disproportionate impacts of climate change and extreme weather events.

Here is an important lesson for students: Dr. Bullard points out that change is never quick or easy, saying, "It took 27 climate summits before the Loss and Damage Fund was adopted as a policy" (Funes, 2023, para. 12). This resonates with Element 1: The Ongoing Struggle for Environmental Justice and Element 2: Learning with/from Others. Thus, while students may be familiar with youth activism movements, which have experienced a boom in recent years, it is also essential for students to know that elders, activists, environmental professionals, and frontline communities have been doing the work for decades, or even centuries, in the case of the Indigenous struggle for environmental Justice.

Global Environmental Justice Picture Books and Activities

Due to colonialism, imperialism, and racism, many communities in the Global South are applying an environmental justice focus to their work. Dr. Bullard also says, "Our principles of environmental justice—which include the safety of workers, the rights of Indigenous peoples, and the honoring of nature—have been translated into half a dozen languages" (Funes, 2023, para. 14). Look at some activities for students that focus on international environmental justice. Picture books are a great way to begin to introduce these concepts. In Table 5.5, each picture book is paired with free teaching resources to support classroom use. There are also lesson plans and extension activity ideas.

Mapping Global Environmental Justice

Oh boy, fun with maps! Students can explore the Global Atlas of Environmental Justice here: https://ejatlas.org/. Known as the EJAtlas, social conflicts and environmental injustices worldwide are mapped on an online interactive platform managed, coordinated, and updated by a collaborative of researchers from the Autonomous University of Barcelona (AUB). In an open-source methodology, hundreds of collaborators worldwide share their

Table 5.5 Picture Books about Global Environmental Justice

Book	Teaching Resources
"Wangari's Trees of Peace" by Jeanette Winter	• Teaching Guide From Globe Trottin' Kids: https://www.globetrottinkids.com/wp-content/uploads/2022/01/wangaris-trees-of-peace-teaching-guide.pdf
"The Story of Environmentalist Wangari Maathai" by Jen Cullerton Johnson	• Lee and Low Books Teacher's Guide: https://www.leeandlow.com/wp-content/uploads/2024/07/The%20Story%20of%20Environmentalist%20Wangari%20Maathai%20Teacher's%20Guide.pdf • The Green Belt Movement Website: https://www.greenbeltmovement.org/who-we-are • Teaching About The Green Belt Movement and Deforestation: https://subjecttoclimate.org/lesson-plans/wangari-maathai-deforestation-lesson (Can be modified for upper elementary)
"Moth and Wasp, Soil and Ocean Remembering Chinese Scientist Pu Zhelong's Work for Sustainable Farming" by Sigrid Schmalzer	• Classroom Guide from Tilbury House Publishers: https://www.tilburyhouse.com/product-page/moth-and-wasp-soil-and-ocean • Reader Guide from Tilbury House Publishers: https://static.wixstatic.com/ugd/cb201d_69c731ab9b554f409c4bceebf47dd558.pdf
"One Plastic Bag: Isatou Ceesay and the Recycling Women of the Gambia" by Miranda Paul	• Author's Book Website: https://oneplasticbag.com/ • STEM Challenge from Arizona State University: https://stemteachers.asu.edu/stem-lesson-plans/one-plastic-bag-stem-challenge • Lesson Plans from New Hampshire Humanities: https://www.nhhumanities.org/oneplasticbag

stories of resistance, struggle, and action. The developers describe the EJAtlas as collaborative and globally co-designed for "activism, advocacy, and scientific knowledge" (Temper et al., 2015).

To begin their explorations and mapping adventures, students can peruse the "About" page to learn about the atlas, the creators' mission, and what they hope to achieve. The teacher can display the EJAtlas on the overhead projector for the whole class to provide students with a tutorial. For older students, they can work in table groups to research different environmental justice topics. Students can focus on specific countries by visiting the "browse maps" tab. In addition, students can explore "commodities" such as uranium, water, land, crude oil, palm oil, etc. Here are some lesson plan ideas:

- **Persuasive Writing:** Students can find a case from the Atlas that interests them. They will then write evidence-based persuasive essays explaining the case and the implications for environmental or climate injustice.
- **Media Connections:** After examining the cases on EJAtlas, students can find a contemporary news article that covers the topic. Students can also consider why that might happen if the media does not cover it. Students can examine legacy media, community news, or student newspapers.
- **Global to Local Connections:** Have students find a case around a commodity listed in the Atlas, such as uranium, water, land, crude oil, palm oil, etc. Are they able to find a connection with any injustices in their town, city, state, or region?
- **Central America Focus:** Teaching for Change (https://www.teachingforchange.org/) is a non-profit social justice education organization. One of their projects, Teaching Central America, has resources on teaching about climate and the environment in Central America (https://www.teachingcentralamerica.org/). One example of global environmental justice is the film "Gold or Water? The Struggle Against Mining in El Salvador." The film examines how residents in Santa Marta have been fighting back in resistance against mining companies from Canada and the United States. Here is a link to the teaching resources: https://www.teachingcentralamerica.org/gold-or-water

These starting points will help you implement Principle 2: Not Just a Science Issue, and Element 1: Engagement and Entry Points across the Curriculum. In addition, we will continue examining Principle 3: In Community with Elders, Activists, and Environmental Professionals, and Element 2: Learning with/from Others. This "plug and play" style toolkit with content connections to art, literacy, social studies, and STEM can also help you take a critical look at your existing curriculum and begin to think of some new ways to challenge the "green status quo" and "green business as usual." I also hope that the content on global environmental justice will help broaden your perspective and enable your students to make connections in their local community and the broader global community.

Now that we have made it to the end of Part 3, consider the following reflection questions as you reflect on your professional practice and curriculum. Also, do not forget to look at the reflection questions for professional practice and the "further reading" resources at the end of this chapter, where you will find materials that can help you extend the learning from this section. There are resources available for teachers, as well as books for both teachers and students. See you in Chapter 6!

Reflection Questions for Professional Practice

Chapter 5 Questions

- Think about your current art curriculum. How might you incorporate some of the ideas from the first graders in the spotlight example?
- If teaching art is not a priority at your school or district, how can you and your students advocate for using art to teach environmental justice?
- What resources does your school have that can help you facilitate an art build? For example, think of student clubs, the PTA, or a very invested group of parent volunteers. Are there any non-profits in your community that can donate art supplies? How about environmental organizations?
- What other compelling questions can you or your students think of to learn about how students can act for the environment?
- Can you enlist your grade-level team, a buddy classroom, or the school to develop your principles of environmental justice collectively? What would you need to make this happen?
- Think about your classroom library. What books might be included on the list of global environmental justice books? Can your school librarian provide other recommendations?

Further Reading: Resources for Teachers and Students

Videos and Resources for Teachers

Equitable Teaching: University of Michigan. *Personal identity wheel.* https://sites.lsa.umich.edu/equitable-teaching/wp-content/uploads/sites/853/2020/09/Personal-Identity-Wheel.pdf

Global Oneness Project. *Do we have a right to clean water.* https://www.globalonenessproject.org/lessons/do-we-have-right-clean-water

ProPublica. *A brief history of environmental justice.* Youtube. https://youtu.be/30xLg2HHg8Q?feature=shared

SubjectToClimate. *Growth mindset classroom posters.* https://subjecttoclimate.org/lesson-plans/growth-mindset-classroom-posters

The Atlantic. *Environmental racism is the new Jim Crow.* Youtube. https://youtu.be/nnF5I7lt6nQ?feature=shared

Books for Teachers

Bullard, R. D. (2018). *Race, place, and environmental justice after Hurricane Katrina: Struggles to reclaim, rebuild, and revitalize New Orleans and the Gulf Coast.* London: Routledge.

Cooper, C. J., & Aronson, M. (2020). *Poisoned water: How the citizens of Flint, Michigan, fought for their lives and warned the Nation.* London: Bloomsbury Publishing.

Finney, C. (2014). *Black faces, white spaces: Reimagining African Americans' relationship to the great outdoors.* Chapel Hill, NC: UNC Press Books.

Méndez, M. (2020). *Climate change from the streets: How conflict and collaboration strengthen the environmental justice movement.* New Haven, CT: Yale University Press.

Sze, J. (2020). *Environmental justice in a moment of danger* (Vol. 11). Oakland, CA: University of California Press.

Washington, H. A. (2019). *A terrible thing to waste: Environmental racism and its assault on the American mind.* New York, NY: Hachette Press.

Picture Books for Student

Berger, M. (1994). *Oil spill!* New York, NY: HarperCollins.

Napoli, D. J. (2010). *Mama Miti: Wangari Maathai and the trees of Kenya.* New York, NY: Simon & Schuster/Paula Wiseman Books.

Paul, M. (2015). *One plastic bag: Isatou Ceesay and the recycling women of the Gambia.* Minneapolis, MN: Millbrook Press.

Winter, J. (2008). *Wangar's trees of peace: A true story from Africa.* New York, NY: Clarion Books.

Chapter Books for Students

Cooper, C., & Aronson, M. (2020). *Poisoned water: How the citizens of Flint, Michigan, fought for their lives and warned the nation.* London: Bloomsbury Publishing (Young Adult Version).

Rhodes, J. P. (2012). *Ninth ward.* New York, NY: Little Brown Books for Young Readers

Rhodes, J. P. (2023). *Paradise on fire.* New York, NY: Little Brown Books for Young Readers

References

Bullard, R. D., & Wright, B. (2009). Race, place, and the environment in post-Katrina New Orleans. In *Race, place and environmental justice after Hurricane Katrina: Struggles to reclaim, rebuild and revitalize New Orleans and the Gulf Coast* (pp. 19–48). Westview Press.

Clements, J. (2024). Unleashing creativity in the classroom: The power of arts integration. *Childhood Education, 100*(5), 12–19.

Funes, Y. (2023). The father of environmental justice exposes the geography of inequity. https://doi.org/10.1038/d41586-023-02613-6

Garaad, Y. (2023, November 16). How Katrina changed disaster preparedness and community response. *Scalawag Magazine*. https://scalawagmagazine.org/2023/11/hurricane-katrina-disaster-preparedness/

National Core Arts Standards. (2015). *National Coalition for Core Arts Standards.* www.nationalartsstandards.org

National Council for the Social Studies. (2013). *The college, career, and civic life (C3) framework for social studies state standards: Guidance for enhancing the Rigor of K-12 civics, economics, geography, and history.* Silver Spring, MD. https://www.socialstudies.org/system/files/2022/c3-framework-for-social-studies-rev0617.2.pdf

Ochoa-Becker, A. S. (Ed.). (2006). *Democratic education for social studies: An issues-centered decision making curriculum.* Greenwich, CT: Information Age Publishing.

Ordóñez-Lancet. (2019). *DJ Caveem's fight to keep our Earth fresh.* National Wildlife Foundation Blog. https://blog.nwf.org/2019/09/dj-cavems-fight-to-keep-our-earth-fresh%EF%BB%BF/

Pew Research Center. (2005, September 8). *Two-in-three critical of Bush's relief efforts: Huge racial divide over Katrina and its consequences.* https://www.pewresearch.org/politics/2005/09/08/two-in-three-critical-of-bushs-relief-efforts/

Temper, L., del Bene, D., & Martinez-Alier, J. (2015). Mapping the frontiers and front lines of global environmental justice: The EJAtlas. *Journal of Political Ecology, 22*(1), 255–278. https://doi.org/10.2458/v22i1.21108

Yes! For Teachers. (n.d.). *Fresh and fly: Denver rapper teaches kids to be gardeners not gangstas.* https://www.yesmagazine.org/education/2014/01/29/fresh-and-fly

Part 4

Digging Deeper—Geography for Environmental Justice Literacy and Action

Part 4 delves deeper into a geography education approach and provides a rationale for why geography education is essential in teaching environmental justice. There are longer project ideas and more in-depth units of study that students and teachers can undertake in their neighborhoods to address local and global issues, including air pollution, transportation, housing equity and redlining, tree equity and urban green space, heat, and community walkability. In Chapter 6, we will dig into Principle 4: Teach across Geographic Perspectives and Element 1: Think Like a Geographer. Learn why geography, specifically human geography, is a critical component of teaching for environmental justice. There is an overview of tools, such as Geographic Information System (GIS) technology, that can help teach geographic literacy and data literacy. There is also an overview of how to do community asset mapping with learners, which can be combined with multidisciplinary entry points across the curriculum. In this chapter's spotlight, learn from my former kindergarten geographers, who demonstrate that human geography is a fundamental subject to help all learners develop their sense of place.

In Chapter 7, we will continue to explore Principle 4: Teach across geographic perspectives and Element 1: Think like a geographer. We will explore a resource bank of free GIS tools and public databases that you can use in your classroom to provide multidisciplinary entry points for environmental justice across your curriculum. We will also explore some examples in context that students can research, such as air pollution, transportation, housing equity and redlining, tree equity and urban green space, heat, and community walkability. There are ideas for continued advocacy and action to disrupt the "green status quo" and "green business as usual." Learn from third-grade environmental justice mappers in this chapter's spotlight.

DOI: 10.4324/9781003620709-10

6

Thinking Like a Geographer

Spotlight: Kindergarten Geographers

"Okay, geographers, today is Wednesday. You know what that means!" said Ms. Waite excitedly.

"LISTENING WALK WEDNESDAY!" *Kindergarteners cheered loudly and pumped their small fists in the air.*

"Yes, that is right," said Ms. Waite. "Remember, we continue learning about the people and places in our school community. We are developing something called spatial thinking. Can someone remind me what spatial thinking means? Let us see some hands!"

"Teacher, spatial thinking is like when you remember where things are. Last week, my mom and I went to the post office. The post office is next to the dry cleaner!"

"Excellent, Lupe, that is correct," said Ms. Waite. "Does anyone else go to the post office or the dry cleaner? Let us see some hands. *Another cluster of hands eagerly shot up, waving back and forth."*

Ms. Waite, when Mr. Kim, the dry cleaner, leaves the door open, it smells clean like soap! My dad likes that place because Mr. Kim makes his work shirts nice and hard! I know it is next to the post office because the mail carrier came in to talk to Mr. Kim and get his uniform cleaned, and it was hard, too, just like my dad's! Lupe is right, the post office is near the dry cleaner!

"Excellent, Mark. Our senses can also help us with spatial thinking. You remembered what the dry cleaner smelled like and saw the mail carrier at the dry cleaner."

"What else is near the post office and the dry cleaner? Does anyone else have any ideas from their spatial thinking?" asked Ms. Waite.

"Teacher, there is a bakery close by! I remember I could smell the pan dulce when I was walking to the park with my mom. My tia said she would buy me a pan dulce after we play in the park," said Tito.

"MMMMMMmmmmmm PAN DULCE!" shouted the class. Suddenly, everyone started to turn and talk to their neighbor. Several students stuck out their tongues to show they were salivating at the thought of this tasty treat.

"Okay, okay, yes, who loves pan dulce, Raise your hand." The class raised their hands and arms in the air; they meant it so much. Huge grins spread across everyone's faces.

"Now, we are going to go on our new listening walk today, and what are the five things that geographers bring with them on listening walks? Let us take out our hands and do it together on our fingers."

"Number One: Eyes. Number Two: Taste. Number Three: Smell. Number Four: Sight. Number Five: Sound."

> Great, now let us look at our graphic organizer. Remember, a graphic organizer is a tool we use to organize our ideas and take notes, just like college students. In this column, we see icons for each of the five senses. In this other column, there is a blank space next to each icon for you to draw and write your notes. Remember, on our listening walk, we stop periodically, and then you can take notes on your clipboards.

"First, let us review the rules for our listening walk. Can someone remind us what the rules are?"

"Hands to self unless you are taking notes," said Carmen.

"Do not stab people with the pencil or hit people with the clipboard," said Ernesto.

"Stay with the class and stay in line," said Allen.

"No talking or shouting in the halls because people are learning," said Lamar.

"When we stop to take notes, you gotta record everything your senses saw and fill the page," said De'Shawn.

"Excellent, my geographers!" said Ms. Waite. "I am going to dismiss you with your rows. Please quietly line up by the door after getting your supplies."

"And we are off!" Whispered Felipe excitedly.

Aren't those kindergarten geographers great? Now, let us look at some key takeaways from the lesson. Element 1 is to think like a geographer. For young learners, an important developmental and social task when thinking like a geographer is learning about the people and places in their communities and how they fit in with this community. This sense of place emerges from a feeling of being connected, whether through emotional, physical, or geographic connections (Relph, 1976). Thus, geographic experiences in elementary school are essential for building a foundation in later life. As educators, we recognize that it is necessary to provide students with geographic learning experiences that prepare them to independently function in society and contribute to the world as informed citizens of local, state, national, and global communities (National Council for the Social Studies [NCSS], 2010).

In Chapter 1, we learned that there are two main branches of geography: physical geography and human geography. The maps and landforms you typically associate with geography are part of physical geography, the study of the world's physical geographic features. This includes landforms, plants, soils, and bodies of water. Contrastingly, human geography is the study of the world's geographic features, like people, landscapes, and communities. Human geographers are primarily concerned with the cultural, economic, political, historical, technological, and social systems. Human geographers also study the intersections of the human and natural worlds, which is our focus when teaching environmental justice. If we are referencing human geography, a sense of place as it relates to human geography would help children understand where they belong in the physical world and also the cultural and social world that they share with others around them.

Beginning to Think Like a Geographer

Why Geography Is Important for Young Learners—Geographers Speak

Why is geography important? Let us find out more! Notably, Yi-Fu Tuan (2001), a Chinese American human geographer, believed that people of all ages need to develop a sense of place to understand their status and role in the world, which contributes to the formation of one's identity. This sense of place becomes a form of "geographic literacy." This geographic literacy is imperative because it involves having the knowledge and tools necessary to protect cultural and natural resources and improve the quality of life worldwide. Geographer Simon Catling (2009) also believes that when geography is taught well, it enables creative opportunities and inquiry, as it allows students to investigate real places and issues, and provides an opportunity for students to develop their active agency, giving them a voice. Geography is also beneficial for helping students to develop their analytic and creative thinking skills because students have to synthesize and integrate ideas from different subject matters, which results in "out of the box" thinking, according to geographer Stephen Scoffham (2022).

Additionally, instead of a relic of the past, geographers want their subject area to be engaging and something alive. Geography is alive!

The Geographical Association (2010) has a manifesto that establishes the rationale and relevance for the field of modern geography as a "living subject." The principles of "living" geography are as follows:

- Directly relevant to people's lives and the world of work
- It is about change and recognizes that the past helps to explain the present
- Has a scale and a "zoom lens" so that the local and global are always connected
- Is "deeply observant" and looks under the surface to dig deeper and identify the causes that change societies and environments
- Encourages a critical understanding of big ideas like sustainability

Geography ultimately helps students develop their understanding of the world, which can be thought of as their geographical imagination. All these benefits make geography essential for teaching environmental justice! Time to explore some initial ideas for introducing geographic literacy to your students and integrating geography into your curriculum and instruction.

In the lower elementary grades, listening walks can be important pedagogical tools for having students begin to actively engage with their immediate environment using a combination of their senses. Students can also make predictions about their walks and hypothesize what kinds of people, places, things, or activities they might encounter in the different areas where they take their walks. On the walk, students can be primed to think about particular sights, sounds, smells, or other tactile experiences. In the spotlight, students took notes on a graphic organizer that had icons. The walk was paused periodically so that students could record their findings in writing or through drawing. After the walk, when students return to class with their notes, several options are available to practice speaking and listening skills. For example, students can engage in a "think-pair-share" activity with a partner and practice sharing their findings using a variety of sentence frames. Students can then write about their listening walks and even draw maps of their journey and explorations. Listening walks can also help students develop their familiarity with the school environment, which is particularly important for younger students who are new to the school. On the listening walk, the teacher can pose two important questions that geographers ask: (1) Why is it there? (2) Why care? Geography is also about discovering answers, and geography emphasizes not only learning from the world but also learning about the world. These place-making activities can occur outside or even around the school or local community. Activities like this can engage children in thinking geographically and develop their geographers' mindset, planting the seeds for a strong foundation that students can build upon and draw from later. Have you ever wondered why geography and social studies are often grouped together? Let us learn more.

What we know as "social studies" encompasses various disciplines, including history, economics, geography, and civics. All these disciplines help students understand the world around them and act. To connect with social studies and local history, I had students interview the school librarian, and we examined old copies of school yearbooks to see how the school had changed over time. This addressed the "now and long ago" standard for kindergarten social studies. My students then wrote about what the school was like in the past, how it has changed, and what it is like now. As a class, we made a three-column chart on butcher paper for students to compare and contrast. Students also compared and contrasted historical photos with current-day school maps and created their own maps of the school. After making their maps, students discussed their map-making choices with a partner.

An additional idea is to invite an alumnus or a community elder to speak to the class, allowing them to share their insights on how the school has evolved. The visitor might bring in some artifacts, old photos, or stories to share with the students. This process of listening walks, historical inquiry, and school map-making helped my students utilize all of their senses, and they began to see themselves not only as geographers and researchers but also as integral members of their school environment. They were directly engaged with place-making and also meaning-making by creating their own maps. This was also a great lesson for English Language Development and math, as students began to learn and use locational vocabulary words such as "next to," "in front of," "behind," etc.

How Elementary Teachers Can Use Geography for Environmental Justice

Here are some additional ideas for exposing students to place-making in elementary school. For students to care about the world around them and the world at large, they must be connected to it through firsthand experiences. Start with simple investigations around the school, which can help students relate to their surroundings and make observations about the world around them. These are essential foundational activities for introducing environmental justice. Students can even take their "geographer's glasses" on their adventures, which were introduced in Chapter 1:

- ◆ **Start a Mental Map Journal:** Children start school with some capacity to locate themselves and navigate their immediate environment. A mental map is their mental image of their home, street, and nearby attractions (Matthews, 1992). These mental maps are developed as children have experiences in the world. As children age and develop, their mental maps become more detailed and accurate. Students can practice drawing mental maps of places around the school or the local town. Students can even keep a journal of their mental maps, which they collect throughout the year, to catalogue their adventures and explorations. Use these mental maps to generate ideas about where students have seen environmental injustices in their community or neighborhood.

- **Plan Field Trips to Local Businesses.** This can include local stores and bodegas, as well as city centers and parks. Students can interview community members to gain an understanding of how the place has changed over time. Students can also take disposable cameras or practice taking a "mental picture" of a certain place. To engage younger students, consider giving them a cardboard picture frame to learn about framing an image in a photo. You can make these for the students, or they can cut out and paint their own frames. If you go around the school or community, have students tie their frames around a piece of yarn so that it resembles a necklace; this way, they will not lose them. To take a place-based approach, students can practice framing the picture with their cardboard frames and making "click" noises like a camera. Students can also take their own "geographer's glasses" on their excursions and wear them around their neck so it does not get lost.
- **Go on a Listening Walk or Even a Smelling Walk!** Take a note-taking sheet, as I did with my kindergartners. This can be a blank notebook or even a camera to document observations through sounds and recordings. This is a good way for students to engage in place-making and meaning-making with their school community. Also, asking students to use their senses can help them brainstorm ideas of where they have seen or smelled environmental issues. For example, in Chapter 1, my students discussed the smell of gasoline they experienced on their way to school. This indicated that they live in a highly polluted and heavily trafficked environment, which served as a good catalyst for further conversations and lessons.
- **Explore a Counting Trail.** In the indoor and outdoor school environments, students can go on a counting trail or a counting walk!. On their walks, students can count the number or frequency of certain objects that they see. This could be leaves, trash, food, etc. Some teachers have a number of the day, and students can practice finding things in the environment that match that number. Counting trails

also have a math extension, as students can practice making tally charts and counting and cardinality.

- **Go on a Shape Hunt around the School.** Directional vocabulary is important in both geography and math. Going on a "shape hunt" or a "shape walk" around the school will allow students to explore essential questions, such as, "What shape is the toy shed behind the playground?" "What shape is the water fountain next to the staff lounge?" etc. Moreover, the teacher can also hide shapes around the classroom or school. The teacher can also enlist the help of other school employees to assist with this. For example, the school custodian or maintenance workers can help. Research has also shown that fieldwork and interacting with their immediate environment can help to promote students' vocabulary acquisition (Ward, 2010).
- **Pattern Trails.** Young children and students are very skilled at finding patterns that occur in the natural world and the built environment. Students can keep track of patterns that they see in the classroom, on the playground, or around the school. Students can create a map of the patterns they observe around the school. For example, consider partnering with a grade-level buddy class for the exercise. Students can combine their pattern maps to make an atlas for the school. This can be shared during a math night or a back-to-school night. Once students begin to notice and track literal patterns in the environment, they will also become more attuned to patterns related to injustice.
- **Emotional Map:** Students can use different colors, shapes, or patterns to represent places on a school or city map where they experience various emotions, which is a valuable exercise in meaning-making and helping students associate meanings and feelings with specific locations. Students can share their findings with a partner in a "think-pair-share" activity, share with the class during a whole group discussion, or you can even help students put their maps together to make an atlas for the class community.
- **Smell Map:** This is a great way to help students associate smells with specific places. Students can use symbols, colors, or patterns and add them to a map of a school, neighborhood, or city. Students can take tally sheets or notepads on their smelling walk and then use the map to record and represent their findings.
- **Sound Map:** During their listening walks, students can use tape recorders to capture what they hear. They can attach the audio files of their findings to a digital map or create a multimedia map using

ArcGIS StoryMaps, which we will learn more about in Chapter 7. To integrate performing arts standards, students can also associate movements with different sounds and then create drawings or writings about what the sounds mean to them.

I hope these ideas spark your imagination and creativity! Here are some additional ways to extend students' learning through more inquiry-based projects related to geographic literacy. Some ideas below for consideration:

- What places in the community are students familiar with? Have students draw their daily route to and from school for ideas.
- Students can deepen their sense of place-making by doing more in-depth explorations of a particular place. Start with something that students are excited about. For example, my students were very enthusiastic about the pan dulce from the local bakery. An idea would be to take a field trip there to see how pan dulce is made, or to invite one of the bakers to come and talk to the students to show them how the pastries are made. This would help students think deeply about the environment and could help them develop increased personal connections.
- Is there a particular landmark in the city or neighborhood that students are really curious about? For example, a statue, a park, a store, or an attraction? This can lead to more in-depth explorations and research. It also provides an opportunity to invite community members into the classroom to share their knowledge.

Now that you have some ideas of how to introduce geography and geographic literacy to your students, let us dig deeper into exploring how Geographic Information Systems (GIS) is an essential component of teaching for environmental justice. As educators committed to fairness and justice, GIS is a great tool to add to your toolkit. It can provide students with real-world data to analyze systemic inequities in the environment. Even kindergarteners can do this!

Data and GIS for Equity and Social Justice

Data, Maps, and Power

Data has a role in either advancing or perpetuating racial, social, and environmental injustices. Thus, data literacy, particularly with a keen eye towards justice and equity, is a fundamental tool for educators and students.

Cartography is the science, study, and practice of making and using maps that represent a particular geographic area. Maps hold a tremendous amount of power, and mapmakers choose what to exclude and include, as well as how the information is visually portrayed to the map user or audience. However, these decisions can have grave consequences. For example, historically, maps have been used to perpetuate injustice and racism, including real estate maps that list communities of color as unworthy of mortgages and political district maps that divide up racial groups in attempts to dilute political power. On the other hand, maps have also been used to challenge and push back against racism and inequality. Let's look at an example from the Black Panther Party and how they used something called "counter-mapping" in their activism.

The Black Panthers used maps to reimagine cities where African Americans lived and struggled (Tyner, 2006). In an attempt to make law enforcement more responsive to communities of color, in the 1960s, the Panthers created a map that proposed dividing police districts in San Francisco, which was based on racial districts. The map can be seen here: https://www.foundsf.org/index.php?title=Black_Panthers. These practices are known as "counter-mapping," which refers to how historically marginalized groups that have been largely excluded from decision-making processes use maps and other geographic data to communicate information about inequities in a visual format, such as a map. Other marginalized groups have also utilized counter-mapping to assert and push back against attempts to erase their history or existence. Here are some additional examples of counter-mapping:

- **Indigenous Amazonian Peoples:** https://theconversation.com/why-amazonian-forest-peoples-are-counter-mapping-their-ancestral-lands-84474
- **The Jim Crow Era "Green Book" Guide:** https://www.smithsonianmag.com/smithsonian-institution/history-green-book-african-american-travelers-180958506/
- **Women:** https://www.routledge.com/Women-and-Cartography-in-the-Progressive-Era/Dando/p/book/9780367245306
- **Queer Communities:** https://uw-geog.maps.arcgis.com/apps/MapSeries/index.html?appid=594c28fb10b84bbda0545a2846fb4d1b

Time for data! Black activists and scholars are utilizing GIS to develop contemporary mapping projects that raise issues of racial justice to the forefront of the public consciousness. While we associate paper maps with the past, many of the maps created today are largely digital. At the foundation of GIS maps, and what differentiates them from the traditional maps one would typically associate with cartography or map-making, is data, specifically geospatial data. Geospatial data is connected to geographic elements that are represented by lines, points, or shapes and represent real locations on our planet. This information is organized and layered. GIS allows the interactions and intersections of scale, space, time, and place to be more visible to the user. Additionally, these digital tools are commonly used in our daily lives today. It could be using Google Earth to take a virtual field trip, Google Maps to navigate around a new city, or visiting the FedEx or USPS website to track the status of a package we expect to receive in the mail.

GIS has enabled us to visualize the past geographically, which helps us analyze and describe how injustices have occurred throughout history. For example, the Equal Justice Initiative has a modern map of historical lynching, which provides interactive updates on the anti-lynching cartography that was started over 100 years ago. Learn more here: https://lynchinginamerica.eji.org/explore. An additional mapping project is called Mapping Police Violence, which was started by data activists after Michael Brown's murder in Ferguson, Missouri, in 2014. It tracks the use of police force in real time: https://mappingpoliceviolence.org/. Now that we understand how mapping and GIS can be used to advance justice and equity, let us explore what this means for teaching environmental justice. Particularly in terms of how GIS can be used for locating and mapping environmental justice sites.

Teaching across Geographic Scales and Perspectives

Geographers are uniquely positioned to discuss our changing planet from a spatial perspective. Dig deeper into Principle 4: Teach across Geographic Perspectives and Element 1: Think Like a Geographer. Elementary students can begin to use their "geographer's glasses" to begin to learn about where things are, why they are there, and how they develop and change over time. The "geographer's glasses" can help students look at different issues and topics from a wide range of scales and perspectives. Geographers are particularly interested in the intersections between these scales and perspectives because they can help them understand complex problems more thoroughly.

A perspective is like a frame (or lens in a glasses frame) of reference used for asking and answering questions, solving problems, and thinking about alternatives, solutions, and potential consequences. Using, analyzing, and acquiring these different perspectives is what makes up a "geographically literate" and informed person. Here are the various perspectives that geographers can employ to examine an issue. Remember, it can be thought of as an interchangeable "lens" that geographers wear in their glasses frames:

1. **Spatial:** The "where"
2. **Cultural:** The "social"

3. **Political:** The "rules"
4. **Economic:** The "costs and benefits"
5. **Historical:** The "past events"
6. **Ecological:** The "human–environment connections"
7. **Geological:** The "physical connections"

Depending on the examined topic and the questions, they can switch out the "perspectives" from the "geographer's glasses." Students can also use the geographic scales as different lenses to examine different perspectives on an issue (Zhao et al., 2020). The geographic scales are:

1. Local
2. Regional
3. Global

In Chapter 1, we used the geographer's glasses to examine the issue of water (Figure 6.1). Now, we will use the "local" scale of tree equity/urban green space. Older students may also use the regional and global scales and then compare and contrast them. Younger students can also use the regional and global scales for longer projects or units of study. Let us put on our geographers' glasses and examine tree equity/urban green space using the different lenses to help us understand this complex issue:

1. **Spatial: The "where"**
   – Where are the trees and green spaces in our community?
   – Where is water cleaned and stored in our community?
   – Where are our school's water fountains?

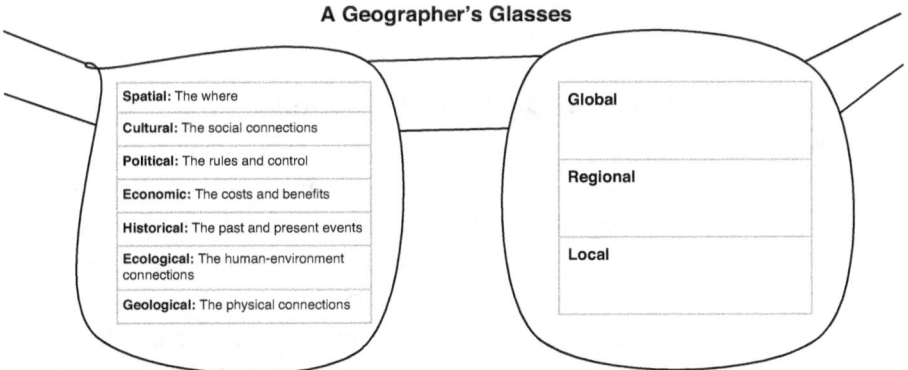

Figure 6.1 A Geographer's Glasses.

2 **Cultural: The "social"**
   - What activities do we do in green spaces in our community?
   - Why are trees and green spaces important to people?

3 **Political: The "rules"**
   - Who controls where the trees are planted in the community?
   - Who plans where green spaces are in the community?
   - Who has access to trees and green spaces in our community?
   - Who does not have access to trees and green spaces?

4 **Economic: The "costs and benefits"**
   - How much does it cost to plant trees?
   - How much does it cost to build green spaces like parks?

5 **Historical: The "past events"**
   - What did people do before the park or green space was there?
   - How long have our community trees been?

6 **Ecological: The "human–environmental connections"**
   - How safe are the green spaces in our community? Can you go there at different times of the day?
   - Do safety and access to the green spaces vary by community?
   - Who owns the trees? Should people own nature?

Depending on the students' ages, consider separating them into groups, assigning each group a specific lens, and having them generate questions related to each lens. Another idea is to have students make research groups. Each group investigates a lens and presents or reports its findings. This could be a good way to integrate digital literacy skills, math, and writing. Let us learn more about why the "spatial" and "ecological" lenses are fundamental to always have in the frame of vision.

Why Data Literacy and Geography Are Needed for Learning about Environmental Justice

In particular, when geographers examine human–environment interactions, they focus on both spatial and ecological perspectives. Let us unpack those perspectives in more depth. The spatial perspective, or the spatial dimension of the human experience in geography, is concerned with "the where." This demonstrates that understanding spatial processes and patterns is crucial for comprehending how people inhabit the Earth. Humans are just one of many species that inhabit Earth, and an ecological perspective involves considering the connections between different ecosystems and human populations. Thus, when the spatial and ecological perspectives are combined, geographers can gain a deeper understanding of both the natural world and human society on Earth. Therefore, when wearing the "geographer's glasses," the spatial and the ecological perspectives or lenses must always be there in the frame of the glasses. This is especially important to keep in mind when teaching about environmental justice, as injustices often involve issues of space, place, and unequal protection. The other lenses (i.e., cultural, political, economic, historical, and geological) can be useful in increasing understanding of the world and more thoroughly comprehending complex issues related to environmental justice. This can be especially useful if you teach about the global applications of environmental justice or regional matters related to environmental justice. Think of the other lenses as supplements that can enrich ways of looking at the world to get a complete 360-degree view!

Time to examine community asset mapping to continue our geography journey and lay a foundation for environmental justice lessons. We will expand on this foundation in Chapter 7, where we will delve more deeply into the use of GIS for environmental justice. Next, we will learn about community asset mapping and its importance in teaching environmental justice.

Community Asset Mapping

The Goal of Community Asset Mapping

What are your community's assets? Community asset mapping is a method for gaining a preliminary understanding of a community's or neighborhood's strengths and weaknesses. An asset is something in a community that can be defined as a valuable resource or strength. This can be schools, green space, public transportation, knowledgeable people, community centers, etc. Considering the assets of a community or neighborhood is crucial in preventing deficit thinking or framing that overlooks communities experiencing environmental injustices. In addition, community asset mapping can help students and youth begin to critically assess their community or neighborhoods as they innovate new solutions to our most pressing environmental problems, such as environmental injustices. These community assets can often be visualized geographically on a map. To initiate this process with your learners, you can help students generate ideas within the different categories outlined below. A broader approach is introduced, first by having students consider assets in terms of both social and physical assets. Then, a more specific approach is introduced below with narrower categories of resources. The approach might depend on students' interests, age level, and abilities.

Examples of Community Asset Mapping
- **Social Assets:** Important community members who have specific skills, perspectives, and knowledge that can help address a problem. This includes parents, students, teachers, elders, community leaders, and others. Social assets can also include community organizations, nonprofits, charities, environmental groups, and activist groups.
- **Physical Assets:** Think of this as the natural environment and the built environment. For example, this could be a community center, sports facility, community garden, park, green space, or beach.

Additionally, students may consider available specific resources. These can include:

- **Food Resources** (ie, Bodega, grocery store, fruit stand, mini-mart, farmers market, etc.)
- **Health Resources** (ie, Hospital, dentist, urgent care, clinic, etc.)
- **Community Resources** (ie, Community gym, church, rec center, park, etc.)
- **Housing Resources** (ie, Shelters, apartments, homes, hotels, etc.)
- **Youth/Student Resources** (ie, Public library, community center, etc.)
- **Physical Space Resources** (ie, Park, local pool, playground, etc.)
- **Students:** Students must remember that they are important resources in the community! They can also be prompted to consider the skills they possess that can benefit the community.

It is also important to note that asset mapping may vary depending on the student's age or developmental thinking. For example, younger students might focus on the tangible things we can see and the immediate environment as assets. They might not be able to grasp the abstract without some guidance from the teacher. On the other hand, older students can focus their asset maps on the numerous social assets and social capital available in their communities. When doing this activity, I am always interested in what students come up with as assets and how they differ or are similar to what an adult would think of.

Examples of Community Asset Mapping with and without Technology
After generating assets and resources, the next step is to put them on a map and represent them visually and geographically. This can be accomplished in several different ways. One way might be to have students draw their maps of the community and then "plot" the location of the specific asset or

resource on the map. Do this on large rolls of butcher paper. This could even be done collaboratively at a grade level for a long mural that can be displayed around the school. This would be a great way to incorporate art, math, and geography standards. Another idea is to use a free GIS tool, such as Google My Maps, to have students create their custom maps. Google My Maps is a web-based mapping tool that lets students create custom maps. Students can add placemarks of community assets and add their lines and shapes. An additional idea is to visit the local library to get city or neighborhood maps. Then, students can "plot" the locations of the assets on copies of the maps using post-its. This can help with learning how to read maps, which is often an underdeveloped skill.

As a way to further involve the community, this asset mapping can also be done at the school-wide level during a back-to-school night. Place large pieces of butcher paper with asset or resource categories in a common area, such as a gym or the school library. Visitors can write their ideas on the post-its and then put them on the butcher paper. It might be beneficial to invite community members, local elders, activists, and environmental organizations to share their thoughts and input as well. This exercise will also demonstrate to students that issues of environmental injustice should be addressed using a community-based approach, as we learned about in previous chapters. In addition, this also demonstrates to students that solutions to environmental injustices should incorporate community input and should not be imposed "top-down" without consideration of the local community's needs or interests. Once the asset map has been created, it can be displayed in the classroom or even the school community as a basis for more project-based learning or inquiry-based learning activities.

Another extension idea to integrate more technology is to have students make and/or host environmental justice podcasts. Older students can write their episodes and scripts and invite community members to speak on the podcast. This podcast can also take an investigative angle as students investigate, research, and talk about issues of environmental justice in their communities. If students are particularly tech-savvy, consider making a Google website that tells the community about the podcast episodes. Students might consider creating a map of assets to display on the website using Google My Maps, which can illustrate the various areas in the city that the speakers represent and/or come from. This website would also be a valuable resource for students to practice digital literacy and writing skills. The podcast would help students practice writing, speaking, listening, and community advocacy. Consider sharing the students' work at a back-to-school night, including it in a class newsletter, or perhaps enlisting another grade to collaborate with your students.

I hope that this chapter provided you with some foundational ideas on how to incorporate Principle 4: Teach across Geographic Perspectives and Element 1: Think Like a Geographer. One of the reasons geography is so important is that it helps establish an "agenda for hope" (Hicks, 2014), nurturing students to develop their critical thinking, creativity, and motivation. Geography also provides many pathways for students to take charge and lead their learning, which can be a powerful driver and motivation! In the next chapter, we will explore how geography is everywhere and how GIS and mapping can be used for environmental justice. We will examine some examples in context closely. Even kindergarteners can do this! Before heading to Chapter 7, look at the reflection questions for professional practice and the further reading section. There are resources for teachers and students to help facilitate geography adventures!

Reflection Questions for Professional Practice

Chapter 6 Questions

- How can engaging in asset mapping help students act for environmental justice?
- What are your community's assets?
- What places in your community have stories to be heard?
- How can you create community partnerships that foster geography and storytelling?
- Can you think of any other curricular ideas where students can practice using their "geographer's glasses?"

Further Reading: Resources for Teachers and Students

Videos and Resources for Teachers

ESRI. *Seeing the future through GIS.* Youtube. https://www.youtube.com/watch?v=y9ptLTiJT6g

The Story of Stuff Project. *Coloring books.* https://www.storyofstuff.org/coloring-books/

Books for Teachers

Dangermond, J. (2024). *The power of where: A geographic approach to the world's greatest challenges.* Redlands, CA: ESRI Press.

ESRI. (2025). *A to Z GIS: An illustrated dictionary of geographic information systems.* Redlands, CA: ESRI Press.

Monmonier, M. (2018). *How to lie with maps.* Chicago, IL: University of Chicago Press.

Yarnold, D. (2024). *The geography of hope: Real-life stories of optimists mapping a better world.* Redlands, CA: ESRI Press.

Picture Books for Students

Balkan, G. (2023). *What a map can do.* New York, NY: Penguin Random House.

B.C. Lester Books. (2021). *Geography: An illustrated A-Z glossary: An introduction to Earth's geographical features for kids (kids geography books).* New York, NY: VKC & B Books

Showers, P. (1993). *The listening walk.* New York, NY: HarperCollins.

References

Catling, S. (2009). Creativity in primary geography. In A. Wilson (Ed.), *Creativity in primary education* (pp. 89–198). Exeter: Learning Matters.

Geographical Association. (2010). *A different view: A manifesto for geography.* Sheffield: Geographical Association.

Geography Education National Implementation Project (GENIP). (1994). *Geography for life: National geography standards.* Washington, DC: National Council for Geographic Education.

Hicks, D. (2014). *Educating for hope in troubled times: Climate change and the transition to a post-carbon future.* London: Institute of Education Press.

Matthews, H. (1992). *Making sense of place.* Hemel Hempstead: Harvester Wheatsheaf.

National Council for the Social Studies (NCSS). (2010). *National curriculum standards for social studies: A framework for teaching, learning, and assessment.* Atlanta, GA: NCSS Publications.

Relph, E. (1976). *Place and placelessness* (Vol. 67, p. 45). London: Pion.

Scoffham, S. (2022). Geography and creativity: Developing joyful and imaginative learners. In *Contemporary issues in primary education* (pp. 21–33). Routledge.

Tuan, Y.-F. (2001). *Space and place: The perspectives of experience* (5th ed.). Minneapolis: University of Minnesota Press.

Tyner, J. A. (2006). "Defend the ghetto": Space and the urban politics of the Black Panther Party. *Annals of the Association of American Geographers, 96*(1), 105–118.

Ward, H. (2010). *Learning for sustainability in schools: Effective pedagogies.* Godalming: WWF.

Zhao, J., Simpson, M., Wallgrün, J. O., et al. (2020). Exploring the effects of geographic scale on spatial learning. *Cognitive Research, 5,* 14. https://doi.org/10.1186/s41235-020-00214-9

7

GIS and Mapping for Environmental Justice

Spotlight: Third-Grade Environmental Justice Mappers

"Okay, class, let us continue our lesson about the Memphis sanitation strike," said Mr. Yamamoto.

> Remember, we have been learning about the important role sanitation workers play in the Environmental Justice Movement, and we read the book, Memphis, Martin, and the Mountaintop: The Sanitation Strike of 1968 by Alice Faye Duncan. Can someone remind us why the role of sanitation workers is so important?

"Mr. Yamamoto," said De'Andre, "the sanitation workers gotta keep the city clean and pick up all the trash from people's homes. They drive around in their big truck."

"Excellent, De'Andre. Can someone else remind me why they went on strike in Memphis in 1968?"

Peter raised his hand. "It is because one of the workers was killed when his truck broke down. It was not safe. We learned that it is called working conditions."

Nicole said, "The city did not care because the sanitation workers were Black. So the workers went on strike with a union."

"And Martin Luther King Jr. said, 'all labor has dignity.' That means that no matter if someone is the company president or the janitor, what they do matters," said Dominique with an emphatic nod.

DOI: 10.4324/9781003620709-12

"Excellent third graders," said Mr. Yamamoto. *"That brings us to our research project for this unit. Today, we are going to be city planners. We will research what days of the week garbage day is in different city areas and plot it on this map."*

"Here is a blown-up map of the city that I got from the library. Each table group gets a copy of the map. Table groups are assigned a specific neighborhood. Table groups will research the following on the city's website:"

- *The day of the week the garbage is picked up in the neighborhood*
- *Find the boundaries of the neighborhood (the streets) and color in the boundaries on the map*
- *If several trucks have different routes in the neighborhood, label them on the map (e.g., assign different colors to different lines for different trucks). Here are some post-its to use as well*
- *Label different landmarks in the neighborhood if there are any (e.g., Parks, etc.).*

"When everyone is finished, table groups will share findings with the class. Tomorrow, we will research the salaries of sanitation workers in our city and compare them to those in other cities. Let us get started!"

Let us unpack some key takeaways from the third-grade environmental justice mappers. This spotlight example builds upon some of the lesson ideas from teaching the Memphis Sanitation Strike, which were provided in Chapter 1. First, students learned about the Memphis Sanitation Strike by reading *Memphis, Martin, and the Mountaintop: The Sanitation Strike of 1968* by Alice Faye Duncan. Next, they engaged with the lesson activities provided in Chapter 1, which are aligned with the Common Core literacy standards. In the spotlight, Mr. Yamamoto added a mapping activity, which is key to understanding the important role that sanitation workers play in the Environmental Justice Movement. This addresses Principle 4: Teach across Geographic Perspectives, and Element 1: Think Like a Geographer.

In this activity, Mr. Yamamoto used an enlarged city map he obtained from the city library. Students then completed their activity by hand, using colors and post-its to identify the boundaries of the garbage routes. If your students prefer to use technology, they can also complete this activity in Google My Maps. Google My Maps is a web-based mapping tool in Google Workspace that enables users to create their custom maps by adding text, marking locations, and incorporating images and videos. These maps can be shared with others and are helpful for collaboration. Another idea would be to use ArcGIS StoryMaps. StoryMaps combines digital mapping with storytelling. Students can add multimedia content, narrative text, and maps. These StoryMaps can also be shared to display and disseminate findings. For example, to illustrate another connection to literacy standards, students can choose to interview sanitation workers in their city and share their findings with the city's Sanitation or Public Works Department to advocate for the importance of sanitation workers in the Environmental Justice Movement. Another idea would be to have a sanitation worker visit the class and share with the students about their daily route and the truck they use.

Remember the "geographer's glasses," from Chapters 1 and 6? This is another great opportunity to reintroduce this to students! In this activity, students will use the following lenses: spatial (the "where") and economic (the costs and benefits). To add to the historical (past events), students can investigate the salaries of sanitation workers in Memphis since the strike and how they have changed over time. Older students could even conduct a salary analysis by considering different geographic scales and comparing their salaries locally and regionally. Now that you have some initial ideas, let us put on our "geographer's glasses" and take a closer look at some examples of how you can use geography, Geographic Information System (GIS), and mapping to teach about environmental justice!

Cultivating an Environmental Justice Literacy with Real GIS and Geographic Data

Overview of GIS Tools and Mapping

Did you ever think "cool" and "geography" could appear in the same sentence? Well, geography IS cool! Geography and "thinking like a geographer" are also fundamental to understanding the role of space and place in environmental injustices. In particular, tools like GIS technology enable students to view a problem in new ways, which enhances their critical thinking skills. Also, the national curricular standards in technology, science, and geography education all call for the extensive use of inquiry-based instructional models in K-12 education (Baker, 2005). Thus, GIS is a handy and rich tool that can support curricular mandates in today's schools.

Additionally, the rise of internet-based mapping tools compared to previous desktop models has made GIS increasingly accessible to teachers and students. We will learn more about this! Geographer Joseph Kerski (2022) researches the role of GIS in education and offers the following ten reasons why teachers should adopt GIS in the classroom:

1 **Spatial Thinking:** Students create their own maps instead of just consuming maps that were previously created by others. Spatial

thinking enables students to view the world as a complex system of interconnected systems.
2. **Critical Thinking:** Students must learn to question the data, methods, and maps. This teaches students to critically analyze their sources as a form of information literacy.
3. **Project-Based Learning:** Using GIS, students actively assume the roles of city planners, geographers, and essential decision-makers. Students can use their maps as launching points for wider project-based learning investigations.
4. **Geographic and Scientific Inquiry:** GIS equips students to ask questions and grapple with problem-solving. This is a form of scientific inquiry.
5. **Data Fluency:** GIS helps students develop technological and digital literacy, as well as data fluency.
6. **Community Connection:** GIS can help students think critically about and solve problems at local, regional, or global levels.
7. **Mobile Workforces:** GIS can help students contact community members to capture data for different projects. This type of hands-on work outside of the classroom involves getting outside and using the five senses.
8. **Career Pathways:** GIS can equip students with valuable workforce skills, such as data literacy. Some examples include civil engineer, app developer, conservationist, and GIS manager.
9. **Content Knowledge:** GIS has applications in various fields, including science, social science, and technology. Actively engaging with data and methods in hands-on ways is more beneficial than just memorizing large amounts of data.
10. **Students as Change Agents:** GIS provides students with the tools, skills, perspectives, and content knowledge to be change agents in their communities.

Resource Bank of Free GIS Tools and Public Databases

GIS certainly has benefits that can serve the next generation of environmental justice activists and civic actors! Asking the question "where" also helps students understand the "how" and the "why." That is the power of geography! Next, let us explore a toolkit and resource bank of free GIS tools to use in the classroom. The examples given in Table 7.1 provide a solid foundation in geography, spatial thinking, and the skills required to think like a geographer. Additionally, Esri's cloud-based ArcGIS Online software is available free of charge for K-12 instruction and can be accessed through a web browser.

Table 7.1 Resource Bank of Free GIS Tools and Public Databases

Tool	Purpose	Resources	Standards Connection Ideas
GeoProject	A GeoProject is a great way to introduce geographic literacy to your students. It is a ready-to-use project-based learning activity that does not require a login, and students can begin exploring right away.	• Mapping A Happy Place: Mapping geographic places that make us Happy: https://storymaps.arcgis.com/stories/03e31a0d980b48f3802ee94d9ac49e1a	• Geography • Literacy • Technology
National Geographic MapMaker	MapMaker is a digital mapping tool, created by National Geographic and ESRI, designed for teachers, students, and National Geographic Explorers.	• Launch Guide: https://www.nationalgeographic.org/society/education-resources/mapmaker-launch-guide/ • MapMaker Collection with lessons and resources: https://education.nationalgeographic.org/resource/mapmaker/	• Social Studies • Geography • Science • Technology
Survey123	Create a survey to collect data on places that are important to you. You can map the results! This is a great tool for helping students develop research literacy, enhance math skills, and engage in the scientific process.	• Survey123 Tutorial: https://learn.arcgis.com/en/projects/map-meaningful-places-in-your-community/	• Math, • Geography • Literacy

(Continued)

Table 7.1 (Continued)

Tool	Purpose	Resources	Standards Connection Ideas
ArcGIS	ArcGIS allows the user to build interactive web maps with ArcGIS Online, ESRI's web-based mapping software.	• Check out these tutorials on how educators, students, and new users can build foundational skills for making maps in ArcGIS Online: https://learn.arcgis.com/en/paths/essential-arcgis-online-skills/	• Math, • Geography • Literacy • Social Studies
ArcGIS StoryMaps	ArcGIS StoryMaps combines storytelling with interactive maps.	• Check out this collection for tutorials, resources, and tips for getting started with using ArcGIS StoryMaps: https://storymaps.arcgis.com/collections/d34681ac0d1a417894a3a3d955c6913f	• Geography • Literacy • Social Studies • Art and/or graphic design

Geography Is Everywhere: Using GIS and Mapping for Environmental Justice—Examples in Context

Using imagination, science, and data to solve our planet's most pressing issues of injustice is a highly creative and innovative endeavor! Your students are certainly up to the task! What is creativity? Creativity involves "possibility thinking" (Craft, 2000), solving and asking questions. If you have ever met a five-year-old, you know they ask many questions, so naturally, they must be very creative! This creative process is not static or linear and involves multiple dimensions that include looking inward and outward at our surroundings. One thing that I love about kindergarteners is that they fundamentally understand the connection between creativity, humor, and fun. And stories! Time to zoom in on the ArcGIS StoryMaps listed in Table 7.1, an excellent tool for harnessing student creativity, storytelling, and data literacy.

StoryMaps represent information related to a specific topic and subject in a storytelling format with maps and media. StoryMaps are also really great platforms for students to display and showcase their portfolios for projects or units of study. The digital format makes it easy to disseminate and share student work and findings with broader audiences, and is also used by researchers, policy workers, and government organizations. Using some of the ideas in context in Table 7.2, you can use the StoryMaps to introduce students to the topic, and it can function as a primary source. If you feel comfortable using the ArcGIS StoryMaps platform, you and your students can also create your StoryMaps. There are also some extension ideas provided in the list below. Let us examine some examples related to these environmental justice topics: air pollution, transportation, housing equity and redlining, tree equity and urban green space, heat, and community walkability. First up is air pollution.

Air Pollution

In the first chapter, we learned from my former kindergarten environmental justice researchers who were using tools like Google Maps and CalEnviroScreen to examine air pollution and access to green space. Check out these ArcGIS StoryMaps for stories about air pollution that can be used as inspiration for projects and function as a teaching tool. Some essential questions to ask students: (1) How has air quality changed over time? (2) Where are the areas concerning air quality? (3) Which year had the worst air quality? (4) How can we analyze air quality using population patterns? (5) Do we see a correlation between socioeconomic status and air quality? (6) How do times of emergency, such as a pandemic or wildfire, impact air quality? Check out the different examples of StoryMaps below:

- Air Quality in the U.S.: https://storymaps.arcgis.com/collections/20aeacd852de4ea8b6616a130fb61760?item=2
- Global Air Quality: https://storymaps.arcgis.com/collections/20aeacd852de4ea8b6616a130fb61760?item=3
- The Air We Breathe: https://storymaps.arcgis.com/collections/20aeacd852de4ea8b6616a130fb61760?item=4
- NOAA's The Pandemic and Air Quality: https://www.noaa.gov/office-education/sos/stories/storymap-pandemic-and-air-quality
- My NASA Data Air Quality StoryMap: https://mynasadata.larc.nasa.gov/interactive-models/air-quality-story-map

For extension ideas, students can conduct air quality experiments in their local neighborhood or around the school. For example, over the course of two weeks, students can use apps to collect air quality data and then record their findings in a scientist's notebook. Some ideas for apps include the EPA's AirNow mobile app and IQAir AirVisual. This is a good way to practice math standards, as students can make graphs to represent their data. Students can write about their data collection process or create policy reports and recommendations to provide to city officials about the air quality in their school community or neighborhood. You can also have students collect data in their yard or a public place near their home, and then plot everyone's location on a map to show the data collection locations. Next up, transportation!

Transportation

When discussing transportation, students can explore this topic in several different directions. For example, they might examine transportation equity in their neighborhood. Transportation equity aims to rectify past discrimination in the allocation, maintenance, and development of public transportation benefits and burdens. This can also be linked to environmental racism. For example, in Los Angeles, the communities that are hardest hit by environmental racism are near extremely congested freeways, where the air quality is severely impacted. As educators committed to equity and social justice, of course, we are not surprised to know that the rates of illness like asthma and cancer are higher in these dense urban areas. Here are some StoryMap resources to use as inspiration:

- Transportation: Transit History Overview and Current State of Transportation in Washington Park: https://storymaps.arcgis.com/stories/b816f5ac275842fbadc3ae274db32a14
- Reconnecting Communities and Neighborhoods: Repairing the Harm Caused by Infrastructure Choices of the Past (U.S. Department of Transportation): https://storymaps.arcgis.com/stories/fe16ad-992fc949e5b3d9f8d56659f9db

As an extension idea, if transportation equity is an issue in your local city or neighborhood, students might also look into the availability of bike paths, bike lanes, or walking trails. Students can research subway costs and other transit options. Students can also investigate whether their city has a sustainability office that outlines any climate goals, and if there is a correlation between these goals and their city's public transportation system. Students could also examine the condition and safety of the streets, as well as any service inequities in street safety and maintenance. Now, time to examine housing equity/redlining.

Housing Equity/Redlining

In the 1930s, the federal government created redlining maps for almost every major American city. The Home Owners' Loan Corporation assessed the "residential security" of American neighborhoods. "Security" was a coded way to mean the "riskiness" of the areas for savings, loans, banks, etc. Maps show the grades, and the neighborhoods that were deemed the "most safe" and less risky are marked as green. Neighborhoods deemed the "most risky" were assigned a red color. Not surprisingly, communities of color, immigrants, or religious minorities were subsequently deemed a threat to home value. Redlining and its historical impact are still relevant today. The University of Richmond has a mapping project called Mapping Inequality, which enables users to explore these historical maps and the legacy and history of racial and ethnic discrimination. Check out their website: https://dsl.richmond.edu/panorama/redlining/about. Students can explore how words have power and can shape neighborhoods, particularly the racially coded words of "safe" and "risky." For some lesson and activity ideas, check out Table 7.2.

As you can see, examining redlining offers a valuable entry point to unpack and address numerous issues related to environmental justice. Once students have this foundational understanding, another area to explore is tree equity and urban green space. Let us learn more below.

Tree Equity/Urban Green Space

Young students are keenly aware of inequities in the environment. As you may recall from Chapter 1, my kindergarten environmental justice researchers observed that there are not many green spaces or places where they live. As an extension idea to encourage students to think critically about the issue of tree equity, you can have them draw a map of the green spaces in their neighborhood, if any exist. Like my kindergarteners did, students can use Google Maps to determine the number of blocks to the closest local green space, and then compare it to different cities in the area. Students can compare and contrast the data. For example, my students were quick to recognize that more affluent cities had more green space compared to their city. Young students can also use Google Maps to explore green spaces, as they are color-coded.

Another idea is to use the website (https://www.treeequityscore.org/). Using this website with GIS tools and various maps, students can take a zoomed-out national view by viewing the map of the United States, and also take a zoomed-in view by choosing to zoom in and examine their local city or area more closely. Students can play with the map layers to analyze patterns. This can be done in groups if students have access to tablets, or the whole

Table 7.2 Redlining and Environmental Justice

Resource	Activity Ideas

• ArcGIS StoryMap: "The Lines That Shape Our Cities: Connecting Present-Day Environmental Inequalities to Redlining Policies of the Late 1930s" https://storymaps.arcgis.com/stories/0f58d49c566b486482b3e64e9e5f7ac9	• The StoryMap includes reflection questions suitable for younger students. The teacher can guide students through the StoryMap and display/project the reflection questions whole group to be discussed as a class, or students can work in groups, or journal individually.
	• Some activities to accompany the StoryMap:
	  a Have students draw a mental map of their neighborhood and create a list of words they would use to describe it.
	  b Now, students pretend they are city officials. What words would the city official use to describe the neighborhood and why?
	  c How can the city assessor's choice of words impact the perception or value of the neighborhood?
	• Students can examine historical maps from the local public library and see if any maps of their city or neighborhood reflect the HOLC assessments.
	• Students can examine the following interconnected issues related to redlining: tree equity and tree coverage, urban heat islands, urban renewal, and others. Older students can explore the StoryMap layers to see how the HOLC data can be overlaid with current data about heat islands, etc. These two overlapping data sets provide different scales and perspectives.

• ArcGIS StoryMap: "Pollution and Prejudice: Redlining and Environmental Justice in California by California EPA" https://pollution-and-prejudice-calrecycle.hub.arcgis.com/	• Students can explore the StoryMap to examine the intersection of redlining and environmental justice in California. There is also a bilingual map and webinar videos.

(Continued)

Table 7.2 (*Continued*)

Resource	Activity Ideas
• "Segregation By the Sea: The History of California's Black Beaches By Charles Bibbs (Mapping Black California)" https://storymaps.arcgis.com/stories/2cb611bca15b48efa45e193ee5894505	• Students can use the StoryMap here to examine the history of segregation regarding California's beaches. • This is also a good connection to examining equity as it relates to natural resources and natural spaces, and who has historically been given or denied access to such spaces. • Students can also research the history and story of Bruce's Beach in California.

class can participate during a class discussion. Students can make a case for tree-planting in areas with a tree inequity issue and also examine data related to temperature, pollution, and the urban heat island effect. Many nonprofits have tree-planting initiatives, which is something that students can research and explore as well. If students discover some tree inequities in their area, they can also use the data to make a case to a city official, principal, superintendent, or other relevant authority. My kindergarteners created a "research report" with their data, which was shared with school and city leaders. Also connected to tree equity and urban cooling is the issue of heat. Let us explore more below.

Heat

Has your teaching been affected by temperature changes in recent years? There have been several days this past year when I had to shift my teaching online due to extreme heat in Los Angeles. Whether kindergartners or undergraduates, students are aware of the extreme weather changes caused by the climate emergency. Many have experienced the impacts firsthand, such as overheated classrooms, lethargic school days due to extreme heat, indoor recesses during heat warnings, and power outages. Your student researchers can examine the effects of extreme heat, which include: extreme heat and heat-related illnesses; Precautions to take during times of extreme heat, and how to stay cool in hot weather.

Students can create a map of cooling centers in their city if one does not already exist. An example is the Chill Out NJ app (https://heat-hub-new-jersey-njdep.hub.arcgis.com/pages/chill-out-nj-nearby-app). Students can also create their guides for cooling centers, including a map or a list of activities to help them stay cool during a heatwave. Students can use programs such as ArcGIS StoryMaps, Google Slides, Book Creator, or Canva to share their findings with the school community or their local neighborhood. This is also a good opportunity for students to do an asset mapping inventory of their city or neighborhood's resources that can help in times of extreme heat, which may include:

- Public libraries
- Malls and other indoor shopping venues
- Youth and community centers
- Senior centers
- Place of worship
- Local pool
- Local park
- Local watershed

Another issue for students to explore with geography or GIS tools is community walkability. See below for some ideas.

Community Walkability

When considering how walkable a community is, several key factors come to mind: safety, the prevalence of crosswalks, transportation options beyond cars, and street design. Walkable communities also start with geography and city planning. Here is an opportunity to introduce your students to the career of a city planner, and even invite a speaker to come to your class to talk to your students. Students can research if there are any active safety campaigns in their city or neighborhood. For example, some issues include aggressive driving, excessive speeding, bike safety, and pedestrian safety. By examining recent news articles in the local news or paper, students can identify areas in the city where these issues are prevalent. Students can examine the National Walkability Index using this ArcGIS StoryMap (https://www.arcgis.com/home/webmap/viewer.html?webmap=f16f5e2f84884b93b380cfd4be9f0bba).

In addition, students can look up the "walkability score" of their neighborhood. Students can apply their knowledge of redlining, transportation equity, and tree equity to identify patterns in communities with a "low" walkability score. Students can also create their own "Community Walkability" maps of their routes to school. Students can draw this or use a device to take pictures. Your class can create a StoryMap of Community Walkability or an Atlas of Community Walkability and share it with city officials or school leaders. This is also an opportunity for students to document issues such as uneven sidewalks or a lack of transportation that they encounter during their walk or journey to school. Joseph Kerski, the geographer we learned about earlier in this chapter, has an example that you can be inspired by and share with students, or create something similar for your class: https://community.esri.com/t5/education-blog/how-walkable-is-your-community/ba-p/883382. Now that you have learned more about GIS and mapping for environmental justice. You have ideas to implement into your instruction. Time to conclude by learning to take the next step and integrate advocacy and action.

Advocacy and Action

Two essential questions that geographers ask themselves when thinking about space and place are: Why is it there? And why care? Most geographers would probably agree that geography itself also functions as a place of action, and geographers have a responsibility for creating actionable knowledge. To help your learners act on behalf of our planet and its people, here are some ideas for disseminating project findings to different audiences.

Ideas to Share Findings with Your School

After your class completes some of the projects from the examples in context, take a look at the toolbox of examples below for how you can create different engagement opportunities for students to harness their creativity and problem-solving and share their findings with your school community. The first example is your school's "Mapping Environmental Stories" exhibit!

1 **Mapping Our Environmental Stories Exhibit:**
   – **Description:** Instead of a traditional gallery, this exhibit focuses on how students spatially represent their environmental observations related to justice issues. Consider consulting your school principal or administrator to see if you can host this exhibit in your school gymnasium or library. You can also involve the PTA to see if they can assist and enlist some parent volunteers. Another idea to consider is inviting the local middle or high school to bring their students to the exhibit!
   – **Spatial Thinking Elements:**
     • **Thematic Maps:** Students create simple maps (hand-drawn or using basic digital tools) showing the physical locations where their photos were taken and then annotate the maps with notes, post-its, or observations about environmental quality (i.e., pollution, access to green spaces, noise levels).

- **"Then and Now" Spatial Comparisons:** Students can find historical photos or create drawings to compare their school or community as it used to be in the past with their current pictures or maps, highlighting environmental changes and their impact. Even kindergarteners can do this! Check your local city library for historical maps. When I was teaching kindergarten, I consulted the school librarian for old yearbooks with historical photos. The kindergarten environmental justice researchers loved being historical detectives!
- **"Our Routes and Our Rights" Maps:** Students can map their journeys to school, parks, or other significant places in the community. Students can then highlight areas where they observe environmental impacts or issues (e.g., pollution, lack of green space, transportation inequity) and reflect on how these spatial differences might relate to equity.

– Other Elements to Consider:
  - Printed and mounted photos alongside their spatial representations (maps, comparisons).
  - Tablets, laptops, or desktop monitors with student ArcGIS StoryMaps. Older students can also create QR codes and place them around the room, allowing visitors to access their StoryMaps.
  - Student-written stories that explicitly connect their observations to location and environmental justice themes. This is a good opportunity to integrate writing.
  - Artwork that spatially depicts environmental issues or solutions they envision for specific places.
  - A "Map Your Voice" station where visitors can add their observations to a community map made by the students. This could be a great collaborative opportunity with other grade levels, or even middle schoolers or high schoolers.

Ideas to Share Findings with the Community

Next, time to explore some creative ideas for how your students can create collaborative opportunities to share their findings with the local community or neighborhood. Consider consulting a principal, administrator, or PTA to help make a district-wide showcase. To advertise for this event, the district's social media and communications representative can help with outreach. Additionally, consider posting flyers at local businesses around the school to inform community members about this interactive event.

2. **Interactive Environmental Justice Exploration:**
   - **Description:** This event and community-focused showcase is a great way to encourage the audience to actively engage with the spatial dimensions of the students' environmental justice projects. This can also be a family-friendly night for Earth Month, disrupting the "Green business as usual" and the "green status quo."
   - **Spatial Thinking Elements:**
     - **"Design a Just Space" Activity:** Visitors are given a map of a hypothetical neighborhood and asked to collaboratively design interventions (e.g., green spaces, community gardens, transportation) to address environmental justice concerns highlighted in the students' work.
     - **Collaborative Community Asset Mapping:** Students can display their community asset maps and have visitors add any additional assets they are familiar with, making it a truly community-collaborative piece. Ask the principal or librarian if this can be displayed permanently in the school after the event. This would work well on long butcher paper. Another idea would be to have stations or "centers" where visitors can interact with the asset maps.
     - **"Then and Now" Spatial Comparisons:** Students can ask community members with a long history of community involvement to serve as a "living atlas" and assist them with their spatial comparisons. At the event, community members can be invited to share any old artifacts, yearbooks, or memorabilia that visitors can examine during the showcase. This would be a great way to introduce students to community archiving. Check if your local town has a historical association as well.
     - **Audience Mapping Activity:** During the Q&A, students can ask the audience about their own experiences with similar environmental issues in their neighborhoods, creating a collective spatial understanding.
   - Other Elements to Consider:
     - A "community planning" station with maps and design materials where residents or community members can create suggestions for improvements related to environmental injustices.
     - Interactive displays of any spatial data collected by students. If students made ArcGIS StoryMaps, consider having this

display in a computer lab or in the library, where visitors can interact with the student maps. This might also be a good opportunity to invite your city planner to this event.
- A feedback station where participants can share their spatially informed observations and ideas about the students' projects.

Next Steps

Now that you know why geography is so cool and are equipped with a "geographer's glasses," I hope you see how powerful geography is for teaching and learning about environmental justice and helping your students to "disrupt the green status quo" and "green business as usual" throughout the year. Geography also teaches students to develop a place-based ethic of care for their environment, which is essential for them to take a position of advocacy and action. Geography is also a highly creative subject and allows students to make connections between different disciplines. Now that we have made it to the end of Part 4, consider the following reflection questions as you reflect on your professional practice and curriculum. Also, do not forget to take a look at the "further reading" resources at the end of this chapter, where you will find materials that can help you extend the learning from this section. There are resources available for teachers, as well as books for both teachers and students.

Reflection Questions for Professional Practice

- Are there other environmental justice issues not mentioned in this chapter that your students can investigate with GIS and geography?
- Who can you partner with to share your findings with your school and community?

Further Reading: Resources for Teachers and Students

Videos and Resources for Teachers

ESRI. *ArcGIS Storytelling Tips*. https://www.esri.com/arcgis-blog/products/arcgis-storymaps/constituent-engagement/announcing-arcgis-storymaps-short-videos

ESRI Academy Web Course: Use a Map for Classroom Instruction. https://www.esri.com/training/catalog/649b20a6bb420d4dfff052b9/use-a-map-for-classroom-instruction/

Kerski, J. (2016). *A good map teaches you to ask a better question.* ESRI. https://www.esri.com/about/newsroom/arcuser/a-good-map-teaches-you-to-ask-a-better-question

SubjectToClimate. *Stay cool ELA unit.* https://subjecttoclimate.org/lesson-plans/unit/stay-cool-ela-unit

Books for Teachers

Jukes, I., & McCain, T. (2010). *Understanding the digital generation: Teaching and learning in the new digital landscape (The 21st century fluency series).* Newbury Park, CA: Corwin Press.

Kerski, J. (2012). *The GIS guide to public domain data.* Redlands, CA: ESRI Press.

Liboirn, M. (2021). *Pollution is colonialism.* Durham: Duke University Press.

McKittrick, K. (2021). *Dear science and other stories.* Durham, NC: Duke University Press.

Picture Books for Students

Beer, J. (2020). *Kids vs. plastic: Ditch the straw and find the pollution solution to bottles, bags, and other single-use plastics.* Washington, DC: National Geographic Kids.

French, J. (2019). *What a waste: Trash, recycling, and protecting our planet (protect the planet).* New York, NY: DK Children.

References

Baker, T. R. (2005). Internet-based GIS mapping to support K-12 education. *The Professional Geographer, 57*(1), 44–50.

Craft, A. (2000). *Creativity across the primary curriculum.* London: RoutledgeFalmer.

Kerski, J. (2022). *The top 10 reasons to adopt GIS in the classroom.* ESRI. https://www.esri.com/about/newsroom/arcuser/why-teach-gis#:~:text=Using%20GIS%20in%20education%20helps,complex%20issues%20of%20our%20day.

University of Richmond. (n.d.). *Mapping inequality.* https://dsl.richmond.edu/panorama/redlining/about

Conclusion

It is hard not to turn on the news these days and not feel depressed. Most days, it feels like a constant cyclone of dark doom and despair, with the continuous news cycle featuring headlines ranging from dismantling the U.S. Department of Education, Executive Orders targeting the LGBTQ+ community, attacks on science, defunding higher education, and attacks on teaching true history. I could go on. However, having critical hope and a sense of collective responsibility for human and non-human relations is imperative (Boler, 2013). Central to this hope and collective responsibility is the concept of freedom dreaming. In these dark and dismal times,

> *freedom dreaming is imagining worlds that are just, representing people's full humanity, centering people left on the edges, thriving in solidarity with folx from different identities who have struggled together for justice, and knowing that dreams are just around the corner with the might of people power.*
> (Love, 2019, p.103)

Freedom dreaming is central to teaching environmental justice because, at its core, environmental justice aims to correct and resist injustices and create a more equitable environment for all. Disrupting the "green status quo" and "green business as usual" would not be possible without first imagining more just possibilities for all of us.

I hope that the Principles of Environmental Justice for K-5 Students will help you teach about environmental justice in an accessible way. Elementary teachers are experts at curriculum integration and teaching across the curriculum, and these principles are built upon best practices that you are already doing in your classroom. So consider them enhancements to your professional practice, not additional add-ons! In this ongoing work of imagining and creating more just and sustainable educational landscapes, teaching across the disciplines and equipping students with various skills is essential. An interdisciplinary approach, specifically one that looks towards social justice, is needed because environmental justice is not just a single subject science issue, as we learned in Principle 2.

This book's heart is Principle 3: In Community with Elders, Activists, and Environmental Professionals. Showing that even mentors have mentors, Dr. Bullard, one of the leaders in the environmental justice movement, whom we learned about in this book, mentioned that his work is inspired by W.E.B. Du Bois (Funes, 2023). W.E.B. Du Bois was a researcher, activist, author, social critic, and civil rights leader. A "Renaissance Man," he was also a strong proponent of an interdisciplinary approach, and his research integrated the natural and social sciences. Moreover, he leveraged his research for the benefit of civil rights and the greater good as a co-founder of the National Association for the Advancement of Colored People (NAACP). Ultimately, as even mentors know, environmental justice work is not done alone or in isolation.

Whether you are a beginner to teaching environmental justice or a seasoned expert, I hope this book helps create a community where you can dream of more just and sustainable futures and disrupt the "green status quo" and "green business as usual." As a former K-12 teacher who was a forced frontline worker during the height of the COVID-19 pandemic, I realize that being a teacher these days is far from easy, and teachers are not afforded the respect, a livable wage, and decency that we deserve as educated and trained professionals. One thing that has always kept the fire continuously ignited for me and the hope alive is the realization that I am actively part of the struggle for justice. It is bigger than just myself: I am part of the movement to teach for truth, and the movement to teach for environmental justice. We are in this together!

With hope and solidarity,
—Kimi Waite

References

Bozalek, V., Leibowitz, B., Carolissen, R., & Boler, M. (Eds.) (2013). Teaching for hope: The ethics of shattering worldviews 1. In *Discerning critical hope in educational practices* (1st ed.) (pp. 26–39). Routledge. https://doi.org/10.4324/9780203431115

Funes, Y. (2023, September 19). *The father of environmental justice exposes the geography of inequity.* Scientific American. https://www.scientificamerican.com/article/the-father-of-environmental-justice-exposes-the-geography-of-inequity/

Love, B. L. (2019). *We want to do more than survive: Abolitionist teaching and the pursuit of educational freedom.* Boston, MA: Beacon Press.

Appendix: List of Online Resources and Hyperlinks

Chapter 1

Read-Along Video by Gilder Lehrman Institute: https://www.gilderlehrman.org/history-resources/videos/memphis-martin-and-mountaintop-sanitation-strike-1968

Read Aloud Video: https://youtu.be/4izeyu74lWQ?feature=shared

Author Interview: https://youtu.be/86eZPI9S8aE?feature=shared

PBS Delano Manongs: https://www.pbs.org/video/kvie-viewfinder-delano-manongs/

"Our Friend Larry Itliong" by AJ Rafael: https://youtu.be/f5Rljoi2ArU?feature=shared

Native Land Resource: https://native-land.ca/

"We Are Water Protectors" activity kit from Roaring Brook Press: https://static.macmillan.com/static/macmillan/2020-online-resources/downloads/we-are-water-protectors-activity-kit.pdf

Interview with Michaela Goade: https://www.youtube.com/watch?v=JvT5hsvUc2E&t=

Common Core English Language Arts Speaking and Listening: https://www.thecorestandards.org/ELA-Literacy/SL/

National Council for the Social Studies Curricular Themes: https://www.socialstudies.org/national-curriculum-standards-social-studies-chapter-2-themes-social-studies

National Geography Standards: https://education.nationalgeographic.org/resource/national-geography-standards-index/

National Arts Standards: https://www.nationalartsstandards.org/

Chapter 2

KQED Lesson Plan Ideas: https://cdn.kqed.org/wp-content/uploads/sites/26/2016/12/Standing-Rock-lesson-plan.pdf

Dr. Wright's Work and Mission: https://youtu.be/hiWj9CgXaXQ?feature=shared

Deep South Center for Environmental Justice: https://dscej.org/

HBCU Climate Change Conference: https://dscej.org/project/hbcu-climate-change-conference/

Copyright material from Kimi Waite (2026), *Teaching Environmental Justice in the Elementary Classroom*, Routledge

- **Environmental Justice Storytellers Project:** https://dscej.org/project/hbcu-climate-change-conference/
- **HBCU Environmental & Climate Justice Corps Summer Internship:** https://dscej.org/project/hbcu-climate-change-conference/
- **HBCU Climate Change Consortium:** https://dscej.org/project/hbcu-climate-change-conference/
- **Dr. Robert Bullard Video:** https://youtu.be/ynYHoPntckk?feature=shared
- **Environmental Justice Case Press Conference:** https://www.facebook.com/InclusiveLA/videos/229369202981850
- **Environmental Justice Court Case Timeline:** https://ccrjustice.org/home/what-we-do/our-cases/inclusive-louisiana-mount-triumph-baptist-church-rise-st-james-v-st-0
- **Court Case Press Release from the Center for Constitutional Rights:** https://ccrjustice.org/home/press-center/press-releases/landmark-environmental-racism-case-cancer-alley-residents-argue
- **Southern Justice Rising:** https://ccrjustice.org/home/what-we-do/issues/southern-justice-rising
- **"The Most Detailed Map of Cancer-Causing Industrial Air Pollution in the U.S.":** https://projects.propublica.org/toxmap/
- **"Poison in the Air":** https://www.propublica.org/article/toxmap-poison-in-the-air
- **CalEnviroScreen:** https://oehha.ca.gov/calenviroscreen
- **"Action Research for Environmental Justice in the Kindergarten Classroom":** https://rethinkingschools.org/articles/action-research-for-environmental-justice-in-the-kindergarten-classroom/
- **Connecticut EJ Screening Tool:** https://connecticut.maps.arcgis.com/apps/webappviewer/index.html?id=5adac07c27db40bbabc193af58634e5a
- **Connecticut ESJ Fact Sheet and User Guide:** https://connecticut-environmental-justice.circa.uconn.edu/fact-sheet/
- **Colorado EnviroScreen:** https://cdphe.colorado.gov/enviroscreen
- **Colorado EnviroScreen Story Maps:** https://cdphe.colorado.gov/colorado-enviroscreen-storymaps
- **Community Mapping System:** https://ncdenr.maps.arcgis.com/apps/webappviewer/index.html?id=1eb0fbe2bcfb4cccb3cc212af8a0b8c8
- **Stakeholder Feedback Link:** https://www.deq.nc.gov/outreach-education/environmental-justice/deq-north-carolina-community-mapping-system/deq-north-carolina-community-mapping-system-survey
- **New Jersey Environmental Justice Mapping, Assessment, and Protection Tool (EJMAP):** https://experience.arcgis.com/experience/548632a2351b41b8a0443cfc3a9f4ef6

MiEJScreen: https://egle.maps.arcgis.com/apps/webappviewer/index.html?id=b100011f137945138a52a35ec6d8676f

EJScreen: https://www.epa.gov/ejscreen

User Guide: https://www.epa.gov/ejscreen/learn-use-ejscreen

Six Americas Quiz: https://climatecommunication.yale.edu/visualizations-data/sassy/

Teach Climate Justice from Zinn Education Project: https://www.zinnedproject.org/campaigns/teach-climate-justice

Climate Generation: https://climategen.org/

EPA Report: https://www.epa.gov/climateimpacts/climate-change-and-health-people-disabilities

People with Disabilities Must Be Included in Climate Planning: https://hls.harvard.edu/today/people-with-disabilities-must-be-included-in-climate-planning-and-responses-say-harvard-researchers/

Alliance for Climate Education: https://acespace.org/

Our Children's Trust: https://www.ourchildrenstrust.org/

Bye-Bye Plastic Bags: https://www.byebyeplasticbags.org/

International Indigenous Youth Council: https://www.facebook.com/IIYCFamily/

The Youth Group That Launched a Movement at Standing Rock: https://www.nytimes.com/2017/01/31/magazine/the-youth-group-that-launched-a-movement-at-standing-rock.html?_r=0

Jasilyn Charger Democracy Now Interview: https://www.democracynow.org/2017/1/4/from_keystone_xl_pipeline_to_dapl

Autumn Peltier CNN Feature: https://www.cnn.com/2022/08/09/americas/autumn-peltier-water-protector-first-nations-canada-spc/index.html

Kathy Jetñil-Kijiner, Poetry Foundation: https://www.poetryfoundation.org/poets/kathy-jetnil-kijiner

Kathy Jetñil-Kijiner, Jo-Jikum: https://www.localfutures.org/programs/global-to-local/planet-local/place-based-education/jo-jikum/

Social Media Handles: @Helenagualinga: https://www.instagram.com/helenagualinga/; @veronicamulenga: https://www.instagram.com/veronicamulenga_/?hl=en; @Mayasideas: https://www.instagram.com/mayasideas/

Chapter 3

J. Drew Lanham's Work and Mission: https://www.youtube.com/watch?v=Ox-8tjIhlAc; https://www.youtube.com/watch?v=8eomGJ5BkYo

"9 Rules for the Woke Bird Watcher": https://orionmagazine.org/article/9-rules-for-the-woke-birdwatcher/

Facing History and Ourselves Video: https://www.facinghistory.org/why-facing-history/choosing-participate

Chapter 4

"Alicia and the Hurricane / Alicia Y El Huracán: A Story of Puerto Rico / Un Cuento de Puerto Rico": https://youtu.be/pNjOjzWOpeQ?feature=shared

University of Oregon Hurricane Maria Interview: https://blogs.uoregon.edu/theuopuertoricoproject/

Teaching for Change's Resource Caribbean Connections, Puerto Rico: https://www.teachingforchange.org/books/puerto-rico

Outdoor Asian: https://www.outdoorasian.com/

Latino Outdoors: https://latinooutdoors.org/

Outdoor Afro: https://outdoorafro.org

Indigenous Environmental Network: https://www.ienearth.org/

Indigenous Climate Action: https://www.indigenousclimateaction.com/

The Venture Out Project: https://www.ventureoutproject.com/aota

Feminist Bird Club: https://www.feministbirdclub.org/

Mālama Pu'uloa Organization: https://www.hepfreehawaii.org/news/welcome-malama-puuloa

Mālama Pu'uloa Island Life Video: https://www.youtube.com/watch?v=ZHdg99T9TzQ

ArcGIS StoryMap, The Pu'uloa Strategic Partnership: https://storymaps.arcgis.com/stories/0beb13c4c833420f87eeda3e65b2cdc5

We Act for Environmental Justice: https://www.weact.org/

We Act for Environmental Justice Healthy Homes: https://www.weact.org/whatwedo/areasofwork/healthy-homes/

NYC Lead Outreach Campaign: https://www.weact.org/campaigns/nyc-lead-outreach-campaign/

Coalition for Asthma Free Homes: https://www.weact.org/campaigns/cafh/

Asian Pacific Environmental Network: https://apen4ej.org/

Lipo and Saeng's Story: https://vimeo.com/364407516

Pan Hai Bo's Story: https://vimeo.com/364407591

Catherine Coleman Flowers Podcast Episode: https://podcasts.apple.com/us/podcast/catherine-coleman-flowers-when-listening-becomes-activism/id1459675744?i=1000520584812

- **UNFAO Podcast:** https://soundcloud.com/unfao/fao-talks-phillips-gender-climate?utm_source=clipboard&utm_campaign=wtshare&utm_medium=widget&utm_content=https%253A%252F%252Fsoundcloud.com%252Funfao%252Ffao-talks-phillips-gender-climate
- **Land Back Resources:** https://ndncollective.org/landback/, https://landback.org/
- **UN-REDD Programme (Lola Cabnal):** https://www.un-redd.org/
- **Confederación de Nacionalidades Indígenas de la Amazonía Ecuatoriana (Verónica Inmunda):** https://confeniae.net/
- **Association of Indigenous Peul Women and Peoples of Chad (Hindou Oumarou Ibrahim):** http://www.afpat.net/
- **Tebtebba-Indigenous Peoples' International Centre for Policy Research and Education (Grace Balawag):** https://www.tebtebba.org/
- **Trouble in the Water Music Video:** https://youtu.be/qDUY3eXv-UY?feature=shared
- **Billie Eilish Music Video Discussion (All the Good Girls Go to Hell):** https://youtu.be/KZYDUw37Js0?feature=shared
- **Ocean Eyes Music Video:** https://youtu.be/viimfQi_pUw?feature=shared
- **Land Back Music Video:** https://youtu.be/67F7WbcTQKA?feature=shared
- **Stand Up / Stand N Rock #NoDAPL Music Video:** https://youtu.be/Onyk7guvHK8?feature=shared
- **In the River Music Video:** https://youtu.be/I4eosRdP5gQ?feature=shared
- **Earth River Music Video:** https://youtu.be/l9tTdy4OnQs?feature=shared
- **No More Pipeline Blues Music Video:** https://youtu.be/zjoRB7ETaGk?feature=shared

Chapter 5

- **Favianna's Artwork:** https://s3.amazonaws.com/favianna-staging/resources/files/f962ce310bae42d7abc9061d95c44437.pdf
- **Social and Environmental Justice Poster Tutorial:** https://www.youtube.com/watch?v=-88O4ISw8Gk
- **Favianna's Shapes:** https://s3.amazonaws.com/favianna-staging/resources/files/b0ce8a1e42f94bb49a52c66194cbfdb6.pdf
- **DJ Caveem:** https://www.chefietef.com/
- **Biomimicz Album:** https://djcavem.bandcamp.com/album/biomimicz
- **Pull Up on the Gate Music Video:** https://youtu.be/ETr8z03Typc?feature=shared
- **Tree Equity:** https://www.treeequityscore.org/

- **Congressional Black Caucus Hurricane Katrina Press Conference on CSPAN:** https://www.c-span.org/search/?For=congressional%20black%20caucus%20katrina
- **Hurricane Katrina Art Lesson Ideas:** https://seldallas.org/unit-12-skill-building-marvelous-cornelius/
- **Teaching Books Curricular Resources:** https://school.teachingbooks.net/tb.cgi?tid=29374
- **STEM and ELA Hurricane Katrina Lesson Plan:** https://wp.wpi.edu/iamstem/2023/08/16/grade-4-a-storm-called-katrina/
- **Coquíes and the Taino people:** https://folkways.si.edu/el-coqui/music/tools-for-teaching/smithsonian
- **Other Hurricane Maria Lesson Plan Ideas:** https://www.learningtogive.org/resources/coquies-still-sing
- **Haiti Earthquake Teaching Resources:** http://briefings.dadeschools.net/files/100148_haiti_earthquake_instructional_resources.pdf
- **The Aid Dilemma:** https://www.pbs.org/wgbh/pages/frontline/teach/haitiaid/lesson.html
- **Teen Fights for Toxic Waste Cleanup (PBS):** https://thinktv.pbslearningmedia.org/resource/envh10.sci.life.eco.superfund/teen-fights-for-toxic-waste-cleanup/
- **Teen Maps Contaminants from Coal Plant (PBS):** https://thinktv.pbslearningmedia.org/resource/envh10.health.coalmap/teen-maps-contaminants-from-a-coal-plant/
- **Pacific Climate Warriors Rally:** https://www.youtube.com/watch?v=CjFA0PYeeK0&t=2s
- **EPA Website:** https://www.epa.gov/superfund
- **EPA Superfund Site Search Page:** https://www.epa.gov/superfund
- **First National People of Color Environmental Leadership Summit Documentary:** https://youtu.be/fo9uaWbhpPc?feature=shared
- **Summit's Proceedings:** https://rescarta.ucc.org/jsp/RcWebImageViewer.jsp?doc_id=32092eb9-294e-4f6e-a880-17b8bbe02d88/OhClUCC0/00000001/00000070&pg_seq=1&search_doc=
- **Summit 30th Anniversary Celebration:** https://www.ucc.org/30th-anniversary-the-first-national-people-of-color-environmental-leadership-summit/
- **17 Principles of Environmental Justice:** http://lvejo.org/wp-content/uploads/2015/04/ej-jemez-principles.pdf
- **Teaching Guide from Globe Trottin' Kids:** https://www.globetrottinkids.com/wp-content/uploads/2022/01/wangaris-trees-of-peace-teaching-guide.pdf

- **Lee and Low Books Teacher's Guide:** https://www.leeandlow.com/wp-content/uploads/2024/07/The%20Story%20of%20Environmentalist%20Wangari%20Maathai%20Teacher's%20Guide.pdf
- **The Green Belt Movement Website:** https://www.greenbeltmovement.org/who-we-are
- **Teaching about the Green Belt Movement and Deforestation:** https://subjecttoclimate.org/lesson-plans/wangari-maathai-deforestation-lesson
- **Tilbury House Publishers Classroom Guide:** https://www.tilburyhouse.com/product-page/moth-and-wasp-soil-and-ocean
- **Tilbury House Publishers Reader Guide:** https://static.wixstatic.com/ugd/cb201d_69c731ab9b554f409c4bceebf47dd558.pdf
- **Miranda Paul's Book Website:** https://oneplasticbag.com/
- **Arizona State University STEM Challenge:** https://stemteachers.asu.edu/stem-lesson-plans/one-plastic-bag-stem-challenge
- **New Hampshire Humanities Lesson Plans:** https://www.nhhumanities.org/oneplasticbag
- **Global Atlas of Environmental Justice:** https://ejatlas.org/
- **Teaching for Change:** https://www.teachingforchange.org/
- **Teaching Central America:** https://www.teachingcentralamerica.org/.
- **"Gold or Water? The Struggle Against Mining in El Salvador" Teaching Resources:** https://www.teachingcentralamerica.org/gold-or-water

Chapter 6

- **Black Panthers Map:** https://www.foundsf.org/index.php?title=Black_Panthers
- **Indigenous Amazonian Peoples Counter-Mapping:** https://theconversation.com/why-amazonian-forest-peoples-are-counter-mapping-their-ancestral-lands-84474
- **The Jim Crow Era "Green Book" Guide Counter-Mapping:** https://www.smithsonianmag.com/smithsonian-institution/history-green-book-african-american-travelers-180958506/
- **Women Counter-Mapping:** https://www.routledge.com/Women-and-Cartography-in-the-Progressive-Era/Dando/p/book/9780367245306
- **Queer Communities Counter-Mapping:** https://uw-geog.maps.arcgis.com/apps/MapSeries/index.html?appid=594c28fb10b84bbda0545a2846fb4d1b
- **Equal Justice Initiative Historical Lynching Map:** https://lynchinginamerica.eji.org/explore
- **Mapping Police Violence:** https://mappingpoliceviolence.org/

Chapter 7

Mapping a Happy Place: https://storymaps.arcgis.com/stories/03e31a0d980b48f3802ee94d9ac49e1a

National Geographic MapMaker Launch Guide: https://www.nationalgeographic.org/society/education-resources/mapmaker-launch-guide/

MapMaker Lessons and Resources: https://education.nationalgeographic.org/resource/mapmaker/

Survey123 Tutorial: https://learn.arcgis.com/en/projects/map-meaningful-places-in-your-community/

ArcGIS Online: https://learn.arcgis.com/en/paths/essential-arcgis-online-skills/

ArcGIS StoryMaps: https://storymaps.arcgis.com/collections/d34681ac0d1a417894a3a3d955c6913f

Air Quality in the U.S. Story Map: https://storymaps.arcgis.com/collections/20aeacd852de4ea8b6616a130fb61760?item=2

Global Air Quality Story Map: https://storymaps.arcgis.com/collections/20aeacd852de4ea8b6616a130fb61760?item=3

The Air We Breathe Story Map: https://storymaps.arcgis.com/collections/20aeacd852de4ea8b6616a130fb61760?item=4

NOAA's the Pandemic and Air Quality Story Map: https://www.noaa.gov/office-education/sos/stories/storymap-pandemic-and-air-quality

My NASA Data Air Quality StoryMap: https://mynasadata.larc.nasa.gov/interactive-models/air-quality-story-map

Transit History Overview and Current State of Transportation in Washington Park: https://storymaps.arcgis.com/stories/b816f5ac275842fbadc3ae274db32a14

Repairing the Harm Caused by Infrastructure Choices of the Past (U.S. Department of Transportation): https://storymaps.arcgis.com/stories/fe16ad992fc949e5b3d9f8d56659f9db

University of Richmond Mapping Inequality: https://dsl.richmond.edu/panorama/redlining/about

Connecting Present-Day Environmental Inequalities to Redlining Policies of the Late 1930s StoryMap: https://storymaps.arcgis.com/stories/0f58d49c566b486482b3e64e9e5f7ac9

Redlining and Environmental Justice in California by California EPA StoryMap: https://pollution-and-prejudice-calrecycle.hub.arcgis.com/

The History of California's Black Beaches StoryMap by Charles Bibbs: https://storymaps.arcgis.com/stories/2cb611bca15b48efa45e193ee5894505

Tree Equity: https://www.treeequityscore.org/
Chill Out NJ App: https://heat-hub-new-jersey-njdep.hub.arcgis.com/pages/chill-out-nj-nearby-app
National Walkability Index StoryMap: https://www.arcgis.com/home/webmap/viewer.html?webmap=f16f5e2f84884b93b380cfd4be9f0bba
Community Walkability by Joseph Kerski: https://community.esri.com/t5/education-blog/how-walkable-is-your-community/ba-p/883382

For Product Safety Concerns and Information please contact our EU
representative GPSR@taylorandfrancis.com
Taylor & Francis Verlag GmbH, Kaufingerstraße 24, 80331 München, Germany

www.ingramcontent.com/pod-product-compliance
Lightning Source LLC
Chambersburg PA
CBHW080837230426
43665CB00021B/2871